PRESENTED TO

Michael

FROM

Dad & Mom

Ellie Claire
Hachette Book Group
1290 Avenue of the Americas, New York, NY 10104

ellieclaire.com
instagram.com/ellieclairegifts

First edition: November 2018

Ellie Claire is a division of Hachette Book Group, Inc. The Ellie Claire name and logo are trademarks of Hachette Book Group, Inc.

The publisher is not responsible for websites (or their content) that are not owned by the publisher.

"Promises and Prayers" is a registered trademark of Worthy Media, Inc.

All Scripture quotations, unless otherwise indicated, are taken from the Holy Bible, New International Version®, NIV®. Copyright ©1973, 1978, 1984, 2011 by Biblica, Inc. Used by permission of Zondervan. All rights reserved worldwide. www.zondervan.com. The "NIV" and "New International Version" are trademarks registered in the United States Patent and Trademark Office by Biblica, Inc.™ | Scripture quotations marked KJV are taken from the King James Version of the Bible. | Scripture quotations marked MSG are taken from *THE MESSAGE*, copyright © 1993, 1994, 1995, 1996, 2000, 2001, 2002 by Eugene H. Peterson. Used by permission of NavPress. All rights reserved. Represented by Tyndale House Publishers, Inc. | Scripture quotations marked ESV are taken from the ESV® Bible (The Holy Bible, English Standard Version®), copyright © 2001 by Crossway, a publishing ministry of Good News Publishers. Used by permission. All rights reserved.

Names and certain details mentioned in this book have been changed to protect the privacy of others.

Print book interior design by Bart Dawson.

Library of Congress Control Number: 2017960762

ISBN: 978-1-68397-247-1 (Leatherluxe®), 978-1-68397-229-7 (ebook)

Printed in China

APS

12 11 10 9 8

PROMISES AND PRAYERS® FOR

MEN

LAWRENCE W. WILSON

In Memory of
Uriah L. Wilson

READ THIS FIRST

Most of the time, reading a men's devotional makes me queasy, as if I'd just swallowed a dozen jelly donuts. They're that syrupy. Many are filled with truisms and trite sayings, sticky-sweet pabulum about how prayer works and how every bad thing is really a good thing in disguise, and if I'll just believe big and act bold God will make the garbage in my life taste like ice cream. My system can't handle the sugar. I get a head rush, then a sick stomach, and then I feel really tired.

What about my daughter, who died at only five months of age?

What about that time I lost my job and had to vacate my house in sixty days?

What about the four major surgeries and the divorce and the runaway teenager and the totaled cars and the "You're not my real dad"?

Why are we afraid to talk plainly about the things men deal with all the time—the pressure to succeed, the stress of managing money, fear of failure, anxiety about relationships, regret, guilt, boredom, anger?

I wonder if we sugarcoat these issues because we fear,

deep down, that God can't handle them. Or that we can't. Or that if we ask one tough question about sex then this whole thing we call faith will crumble like a sandcastle in the tide.

It won't, you know.

The promises of Scripture are as good for grown men as they are for little children. The things we know about life, about ourselves, about God are just as valid in this post-Christian, postmodern, post-everything world as they were ten thousand years ago. There's no reason not to ask tough questions and hope for solid answers. The promises offered here are not slender reeds for hesitant souls who are fearful of testing them with real weight. They are carbon-steel jack stands, capable of supporting enormous burdens, durable, dependable, indestructible. If the truth is brutal, there's nothing more rugged than the Word of God.

It's likely that you've picked up this book because you're being crushed by one of these enormous burdens right now and are ready for some relief. If so, you've come to the right place. I invite you to feed on this book and the promises it contains. You can read it cover to cover, or you can browse for the subjects that appeal to you, or read an entry a day for forty days. Either way, I welcome you on this journey to discover God in a deeper way. As you explore these timeworn promises and pray these simple prayers, you will learn what strong, determined, able men have known for centuries: you can throw all your weight on God, because He really does care for you (1 Peter 5:7).

DAY 1

EMBRACE
THE NEW YOU

THE PROMISE

You are forever changed.

Therefore, if anyone is in Christ,
the new creation has come:
The old has gone, the new is here!

2 CORINTHIANS 5:17

Reunions are a form of time travel. These gatherings of family, former classmates, or fellow soldiers have a way of turning back the calendar, transporting grown men and women to a simpler time. A forty-year-old man arrives at a family reunion perhaps as a husband and father, a successful businessman, or a skilled tradesman or professional. Yet when he sits at the picnic table eating hotdogs, trading stories with siblings and cousins, he is once again the baby of the family.

A class reunion can have a similar effect, which is why I avoided them for many years after high school. I didn't care for the person I was back then, so I had no desire to return to the time when I was a little younger than everyone else, not quite as smart, and barely able to keep up. I liked to think that the years and the miles, the diplomas and the children, even the gray hairs, were evidence that I'd changed. I was no longer the gawky kid who mispronounced "Tybalt" while auditioning for *Romeo and Juliet* and was too slow to make the basketball team. At least I hoped I wasn't the same person. To attend a reunion would put that theory to the test, and I lacked the courage to find out for sure.

Former selves haunt all of us in many ways, lurking in the shadows of our lives, ever ready to make an unwelcome entrance. Sometimes they are called forth by meeting an old acquaintance whose very presence reminds us of an embarrassing incident. Or they assert themselves during a heated argument, when a wife reminds us of that awful thing we once said or the selfish way we responded to disappointment. We'd like to think that we're not the same, that we've grown far beyond those childish mistakes. But we're never quite sure. Despite the evidence in the mirror, we can't help but wonder if anything about us is different than before. If we weren't good enough then, why would we be now? Is that awkward teen—or lying husband or deadbeat dad or inept employee—still in there somewhere?

The apostle Paul must have understood our fear of class reunions. Why else would he so emphatically stress the idea that the old you is gone forever, replaced by a new and different person through faith in Christ? The new birth produces a new life. This is the promise of God, His pronouncement upon you: you are forever changed. You are not the man you once were, and certainly not the boy. By following Jesus Christ, you have entered a new life. What welcome assurance that is.

True, you may still display a few characteristics of the old you. The pimply teenager didn't disappear the day after graduation, but there was no going back to high school. You'd ended one life and entered another. So too with your identity as a child of God. Your growth will take time, but this new life is yours for keeps.

After twenty years of gathering my courage, I finally attended a high school reunion. I was pleased to discover exactly what I'd hoped all along. I was different at thirty-eight than I'd been at eighteen. We all were. Despite a few extra pounds, we'd changed for the better.

You have too.

A TIMELY TIP

Looking back isn't going to help you.
Moving forward is the thing you have to do.
McKayla Maroney

TRY IT

When you look in the mirror today,
say out loud,
"I'm not the man I used to be."

A PRAYER

Lord, thank You for offering me a fresh start.
Help me to own this new identity
and live today like the new person
You have created me to be.
Amen.

DAY 2

— — —

LOVE GOD

Blessed are the pure in heart,
for they will see God.

MATTHEW 5:8

W ell, he works at it. He doesn't sit on his hands like some."

I was a young pastor, listening to a conversation between a couple of seasoned ministers. They were discussing a colleague who put an enormous number of miles on his car each year, requiring frequent oil changes. In those days, visiting parishioners in their homes, at the hospital, and even at workplaces, sporting events, and school activities was common practice. Serving a rural parish that covered most of the county, the pastor in question drove tens of thousands of miles a year, which put his car in the shop at least once a month. Hence, the discussion.

"He doesn't sit on his hands like some." Heads nodded in approval, making the implication obvious: it takes constant effort to do the Lord's work. To be a good pastor, you must wear out a set of tires—and probably yourself.

That idea branded itself onto my consciousness, and I

made the decision to be a pastor who "works at it." I would prove my devotion to the Lord by exhausting myself in His service. My family paid the price for that choice for years to come.

Pastors are not the only ones who can feel they're never doing enough for God. Laypeople may also have the idea that they must do more, care more, achieve more, attend more meetings, give more money, forego more sleep, and spend more time away from home to finally win God's approval. We don't want to be caught sitting on our hands when Christ returns. We want to be out there, in the field, working at it.

If that sounds familiar, stop for a minute. Slow your pace, set aside your to-do list, quit looking at your phone and pondering that opportunity to volunteer one more night this week. Hear this: God cares more about who you are than what you do. You are His child, and He loves you. Love Him back. That's all you really have to do.

It isn't that your conduct doesn't matter. Of course it's important to behave morally and to serve others. Both are vital aspects of our life in the Spirit. The problem comes in confusing the order of our salvation. We are convinced that doing leads to being. We think that if we do more for God, we'll become more valuable to God. It's an outside-in approach to the good life. The harder we work, the better we'll be.

That's dead wrong.

Life in the Spirit flows from the inside out. Hard work does not make the heart pure. A heart filled with love for God overflows into loving others, which prompts us to do good in the world, not frenetically, obsessively, or exhaustingly, but with calm confidence and impeccable balance.

Outside-in spirituality is worse than misguided. It is harmful to you and those around you. A friend spent several years as a missionary before returning home burned out, his marriage in tatters. "While I was traveling a lot, working hard, really thriving, my wife was dying inside and I just couldn't see it," he said. "To tell you the truth, I was more in love with the ministry than I was with God."

Busy hands will never make a heart pure. All God asks is that you love Him. Center your affection on Him. Do that and you will have done the one thing that is most needed. That will always be good enough.

A TIMELY TIP

The foe of opportunity is preoccupation.
Just when God sends along a chance
to turn a great victory for mankind,
some of us are too busy
puttering around to notice it.

A. W. TOZER

TRY IT

Take one thing off of your calendar
this week so you can spend more time
in the presence of God.

A PRAYER

---

*Lord, I have sometimes cared about
Your work more than about You.
I've wanted Your approval more than Your presence.
Help me to love You the way You love me
and to rest in the knowledge of Your approval.
Amen.*

DAY 3
— —— —

ACCEPT
FORGIVENESS

You can know for sure
that God loves you.

The Spirit himself testifies with our spirit
that we are God's children.

ROMANS 8:16

If you were to die tonight, do you know for sure that you would go to heaven?" I felt a little cheesy asking the question, but it seemed appropriate under the circumstances. Alex, a thirty-five-year-old husband and father, was sitting in my office asking what it meant to be a Christian. His wife, Maria, paced the hallway, trying to keep two preschoolers occupied. Realizing that I had no time to waste, I resorted to the daunting question from a method for explaining the Christian faith that had been popular a few years before.

"No," Alex said, wagging his head slowly. "I don't think so."

"Would you like to know for sure?"

"Absolutely."

With that I launched into what is sometimes called the Bridge Illustration. It pictures a person standing on one side of a chasm, God on the other side, and a cross forming a bridge between the two. I described the meaning of the illustration to Alex, then asked, "In terms of your relationship with God, where would you say you are right now?"

"About here," he said, pointing to a spot about one-third of the way across the bridge. "I pray sometimes, but me and God aren't exactly tight."

I explained that Jesus's death on the cross closed the gap created by sin, making it possible for us to have a relationship with God. I quoted 1 Timothy 2:5, "For there is one God and one mediator between God and mankind, the man Christ Jesus." Then I asked Alex if he'd like to pray, expressing his faith in Christ. Alex readily agreed, and we prayed together.

"Now where would you say you are?" I asked.

"About here," Alex said, pointing to a spot about halfway across the bridge. "Maybe one step closer."

Alex's experience is not uncommon. Despite their profession of faith in Christ, many men feel they're never quite "in" with God. They are keenly aware of their sins. They've failed God and others repeatedly. Some have been told—by parents, spouses, coworkers—that they simply don't measure up. And they believe it. Despite what they may have heard in church or remember from childhood Bible lessons, they can't accept the idea that God really, truly loves them. In their minds, they'll be like Gandalf on the bridge of Khazad-dûm, suspended over a pit of fire with somebody shouting, "You shall not pass!"

Jesus understood that feeling, which is why He promised to send the Comforter, who is the Holy Spirit, to remind us of important truths (see John 14:26). One of those important truths is that through faith in Jesus Christ, we are, in fact, truly, no mistake, I'm really not kidding about this, loved by God. We are adopted into His family, called His sons, treated to a place at the table, brought near. Our place is with God now. We're part of His family. We'll never be on the other side, or dangling in the middle, again.

I kicked myself for not finishing the Bridge diagram with Alex, and I quickly spat out 1 John 5:13: "I write these things to you who believe in the name of the Son of God so that you may know that you have eternal life." God loves you. He really does. And based on your acceptance of Christ, you can know that for certain. Quiet your mind, open your heart, and let the Spirit speak.

A TIMELY TIP

Though our feelings come and go,
God's love for us does not.

C. S. LEWIS

TRY IT

Write the text of John 5:24
on an index card,
and read it aloud every day this week.

A PRAYER

Holy Spirit, speak to me.
In the stillness of this moment,
cut through the shame and regret
to let me hear Your voice
and feel Your presence.
Amen.

DAY 4

LIVE FREE

THE PROMISE

You are forgiven, you are loved,
and you are free.

That is what some of you were.
But you were washed, you were sanctified,
you were justified in the name
of the Lord Jesus Christ and by the Spirit of our God.

1 CORINTHIANS 6:11

Poor Jacob Marley. Or rather the ghost of Jacob Marley, business partner to Ebenezer Scrooge in Charles Dickens's classic story *A Christmas Carol*. In the afterlife, Marley was condemned to walk the earth shackled with a massive iron chain, each link representing a misdeed done in his lifetime. Since he had been a cunning businessman, cheating and mistreating all with whom he dealt, Marley's chain was long and heavy. His sins were a great burden to bear.

"You are fettered," said Scrooge, trembling. "Tell me why?"

"I wear the chain I forged in life," replied the Ghost. "I made it link by link, and yard by yard; I girded it on of my own free will, and of my own free will I wore it. Is its pattern strange to you?"

Scrooge trembled more and more.

"Or would you know," pursued the Ghost, "the weight and length of the strong coil you bear yourself? It was full as heavy and as long as this, seven Christmas Eves ago. You have laboured on it, since. It is a ponderous chain!"[1]

Many living men carry a similar burden of guilt for the things they've done. They walk the earth shackled by an invisible chain of regret over past sins. It rattles a little when they think of the people they've mistreated, or threatened, or lied to. Some men are literally bound in a prison cell because of their crimes. Others carry weight in the form of consequences for their sin: physical scars, lost opportunities, estranged children. The burdens of the past are oppressively heavy.

And bearing that weight is ruinous. Some carry a deep sadness that prevents them from looking to the future with hope or optimism. Others feel intense anger at their helplessness to change the past or change themselves. A few resign themselves to a life of repeated failure, falling again and again into the same sins, adding link upon link to the chain that weights their soul.

This need not be. In Dickens's story, Jacob Marley promised his old friend, "I am here to-night to warn you, that you have yet a chance and hope of escaping my fate. A chance and hope of my procuring, Ebenezer." Marley offered Ebenezer Scrooge a second chance, a way to avoid carrying the chains of guilt for all eternity. Ironically, the great question in *A Christmas Carol* is whether or not Scrooge will accept the freedom he is offered. Will he see his own need? Will he alter his direction? Will he accept the chance to begin life again?

Will you? You have that same opportunity, made possible by One who has already passed from this life into the next. You can set aside the burden of your past. Jesus offers complete freedom from sin—from the guilt, the shame, and the repeated failure. If you have not accepted this liberty, you can do that now simply by believing in Jesus. And if you have done so, hear this promise: you need not carry the weight of sin anymore. Regardless of what you once were or what you once did, you have been washed, you have been sanctified, you have been justified in the name of the Lord Jesus Christ. The past no longer has the power to dominate your life. You are forgiven, you are loved, and you are free.

A TIMELY TIP

Close the door on the past.
You don't try to forget the mistakes,
but you don't dwell on it.
You don't let it have any of your energy,
or any of your time, or any of your space.

JOHNNY CASH

TRY IT

The next time you pick up a heavy object,
hold it for a moment, then set it down
and say, "Thank You, Lord,
for taking the weight."

A PRAYER

Lord, I can't carry these burdens anymore,
and I'm so grateful that I don't have to.
Thank You for my freedom.
Help me to live in it, and live up to it, today.
Amen.

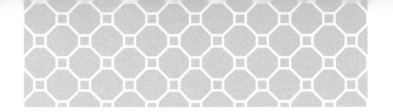

DAY 5

LISTEN

In the past God spoke to our ancestors
through the prophets at many times
and in various ways, but in these last days
he has spoken to us by his Son.

HEBREWS 1:1–2

———————————————————————

T hank you for your sermon on doubt," the handwritten card read. "I have struggled with this my whole life, and it is especially hard now that my wife is gone. I'm glad to know I'm not alone."

The signature was that of an elderly widower and long-standing believer in our congregation. His admission was confidential, I knew. His adult children were all believers, some of them in the ministry. Clearly, doubt was a burden he had carried for some time. Was I the first person in eighty years to whom he had revealed this secret?

The experience of doubt is more common among believers than one might think. Though they often hide it, many, perhaps most, Christians doubt from time to time. I do. There have been notable examples throughout history.

On the Mount of Ascension, standing face to face with

the resurrected Jesus, some of the apostles doubted (see Matthew 28:17). The reformer John Calvin wrote, "For unbelief is so deeply rooted in our hearts, and we are so inclined to it, that not without hard struggle is each one able to persuade himself of what all confess with the mouth: namely, that God is faithful." Renowned nineteenth-century preacher Charles Spurgeon wrote about what he called "the minister's fainting fits," periods of gloom common among clergy in which some are tempted to abandon the faith. Even the venerable C. S. Lewis noted, "Now that I am a Christian I do have moods in which the whole thing looks very improbable; but when I was an atheist I had moods in which Christianity looked terribly probable." If you have doubts about the Bible, about the Christian story, or even the existence of God, you're certainly not alone, even at church.

Some men deal with doubt by smiling benignly through the sermon, keeping their mouth shut at small group, and putting their questions about religion in a lockbox at the back of their brain. They don't want to disappoint their wife or rob their kids of the comfort of faith simply because they feel uncertainty. For others, the tension is simply too great to bear. So they make a break, backing away from faith altogether rather than ignoring their skepticism about miracles, questions about the Bible, and their constant indecision about the existence of a God who invades human existence by talking to people. They simply cannot be convinced.

Of course, nobody can be. Convinced, that is. Faith is not a matter of facts and figures, or forensic evidence, laboratory experiments, and empirical proofs. It is precisely the opposite of all that. Rather than certainty based on verifiable proof, "faith is confidence in what we hope for and assurance about what we do not see" (Hebrews 11:1). It isn't that there is no evidence for the existence of God. The world itself, Scripture, and even our own consciences point to the reality of what we believe. But faith will never result from reason. It comes from a relationship. We do not believe in the evidence. We come to know a person. God has spoken on many occasions and in a variety of ways, but the ultimate revelation of Himself is His Son, Jesus Christ. To know Him is to know God, and to trust Him is to have faith in God.

Sometimes the best way to find something is to quit looking for it. "Be still, and know that I am God," the Lord has promised (Psalm 46:10). Try it and see.

A TIMELY TIP

Faith is taking the first step
even when you don't see
the whole staircase.
MARTIN LUTHER KING JR.

TRY IT

The next time you doubt, turn the tables
by questioning the source
of your uncertainty rather than
the source of your faith.

A PRAYER

O God, reveal Yourself to me.
I don't know if You are there.
I don't know if You are listening.
But I want to know. Speak to me
through Your Word, through Your world,
and through Your Son. Help my unbelief.
Amen.

FOLLOW THE SPIRIT

THE PROMISE

The Spirit will guide you in knowing when,
where, and how to serve.

The Spirit told Philip,
"Go to that chariot and stay near it."
ACTS 8:29

My dad is a preacher, as I was for some twenty years. We come from a family of preachers, nine of us among our extended family. You'd think that would make us born evangelists, the type who share their faith at the grocery store or lead people to Christ while waiting for the light to change. Not so much. We're all introverts and find the prospect of talking about Jesus with total strangers about as appealing as sharing about our feelings.

In an attempt to become more effective at leading others to Christ, my father once took a course in personal witnessing while attending a ministry conference. All morning the instructor explained techniques for starting spiritual conversations, explaining the way of salvation, and leading people to profess their faith. At the lunch break, the eager participants were unleashed on the city of Detroit to practice their craft. Dad took a nap in the car.

Later that afternoon, the group gathered back at the convention site to debrief. Some shared modest successes.

Most were a little embarrassed about their lack of results. Then Dad got a bright idea.

"How did it go with you?" he asked the instructor. "Did you bring anyone to faith?"

A pause. "Well, I don't actually practice these techniques myself," he said at last. "You see, everybody has their own spiritual gift. Mine is teaching, not evangelism."

The fellow was right, of course. Not everyone gets the same gift. Each of us has a different mix of temperament, inclinations, natural abilities, and one more thing: spiritual gifts. Add all of those things together, and you get an individual with a unique calling and responsibilities. While everyone can share their faith, not everyone is called to be an evangelist. Anybody can lend a hand in doing chores, but some people are especially gifted at seeing and meeting the practical needs of others. What some find terrifying— speaking in public—is exhilarating and satisfying for others. We are not all gifted in the same ways, and we are not all expected to serve Christ by doing the same things.

Even so, it can be confusing to determine exactly when, where, and how to take action. How do you know which opportunities are right for you? Should you pound the pavement to make disciples or take a nap in the car? The story of Philip provides a great principle for answering those questions: follow the Spirit.

The apostle Philip was directed by God to set out from

Jerusalem one day, and he encountered an important government official from Ethiopia. The Spirit led Philip to approach the man, and Philip did so. As a result of the encounter, the Ethiopian official became a convert, carrying Christianity back to his homeland. Why did this happen? Because Philip followed the Spirit.

False guilt rises from feeling responsible to do *everything* for Christ. You are responsible only for the specific things the Spirit leads you to do. And when God prompts you to take action, He will also empower you to succeed. If you are led to teach, teach. If you feel called to serve on a mission trip, go. If God leads you to share your faith, speak boldly. He will give you the wisdom and power to serve as He directs.

My dad is not especially gifted at personal evangelism, but he wasn't idle in serving Christ. As a pastor, conference speaker, and international radio broadcaster, he proclaimed the gospel to millions of people around the world for over sixty years. Thousands have come to Christ because he did the work the Spirit gave *him* to do.

A TIMELY TIP

If we function according to our ability alone,
we get the glory; if we function according
to the power of the Spirit within us,
God gets the glory.

HENRY BLACKABY

TRY IT

Be alert for divine appointments
as you go about your work today.

A PRAYER

Lord, I want to serve You, but I don't even know
where to begin. Give me a strong dose
of Your Holy Spirit. Fill me with love
for You and for others, then be my guide.
I promise to follow Your lead.
Amen.

DAY 7

— — —

PURSUE HOLINESS

THE PROMISE

God can change your heart,
and He will.

Blessed are those who hunger and thirst
for righteousness, for they will be filled.
MATTHEW 5:6

Mike was one of the biggest men I've ever known. He was probably fifty years old, maybe six-foot-five and about three hundred pounds. Grizzled whiskers decorated his chin long before the invention of the stubble razor. His sore knees and knotted hands gave evidence of a life spent at hard labor. "Bull work is all I've ever done," he once told me.

Mike wasn't much for talking, but at one church meeting the preacher asked if anybody had a testimony, and Mike was the first to his feet. "I think everybody knows my story," he said, "but maybe not. I was a drunk and the worst guy I knew. I got in a bar fight about every week, and I didn't treat my wife too good neither." Marjorie nodded approval in the seat beside him. "But Jesus got ahold of me," Mike went on, just the hint of a crack in his voice. "I ain't been the same since. He saved my life, and my wife stood by me." Marge nodded again, vigorously. "I ain't had a drink in over twenty years, and I thank God for what He done for me."

Then Mike sat down. That pretty much ended the testimony time. No one wanted to top that.

Thirty years have passed since Mike shared that story. In the intervening decades, I've heard fewer and fewer testimonies from men who were not only forgiven for sin but also enabled to overcome it. More often I hear testimonies of struggles from men who deal repeatedly with bad habits they simply can't break. These are sincere Christian men who have become so weary of their inability to live righteously that they've simply given up trying. Some have cut a deal with the devil, saying, in effect, "Okay, you can have that part of me, but no more. I'll be a decent guy in most ways, but in the area of (sex, booze, anger, whatever), you win."

Frankly, I don't blame them for being discouraged. We're taught from a young age that real men get the job done. Whatever it is, you power through it. You work hard, you play hard, you take the pain. And if you gut it out long enough, you win. But that doesn't work with sin. There is no level of willpower that can defeat an addiction to sex or alcohol or gambling. Self-discipline may get you to the gym on a December morning or keep you making sales calls until you hit your bonus, but it will never eradicate your desire to do that one thing that has a hold on you. Sin is a problem you cannot solve.

But God can.

The apostle John wrote that if we "confess our sins, he

is faithful and just and will forgive us our sins and purify us from all unrighteousness" (1 John 1:9). Don't miss that last part, about cleansing. David, the great king of Israel who had a knack for both winning and sinning, wrote, "Wash away all my iniquity and cleanse me from my sin. . . . Create in me a pure heart, O God" (Psalm 51:2, 10). He was talking about forgiveness, yes, but something more. David didn't want to be *only* forgiven for sin. He wanted to be rid of it. And here's the promise of Jesus: blessed are you when the deepest longing of your heart is to be clean, pure, right—because you will be. The Spirit can do in you what you cannot do for yourself. And one of these days, you'll be able to stand, like Mike, and say, "But Jesus got ahold of me, and I ain't been the same since."

A TIMELY TIP

Do not strive in your own strength;
cast yourself at the feet of the Lord Jesus,
and wait upon Him in the sure confidence
that He is with you, and works in you.

ANDREW MURRAY

TRY IT

Tell a trusted friend about your struggle
with sin, and ask him to pray with you.

A PRAYER

Lord, I'm tired of doing this on my own.
I've tried to make myself a better person, but I can't.
Through the power of Your Spirit, forgive me,
cleanse me, and make me new.
I'm ready, really ready, for change.
Amen.

DAY 8

- - -

RECEIVE LOVE

THE PROMISE

God loves you always,
even when others don't.

The LORD is close to the brokenhearted
and saves those who are crushed in spirit.

PSALM 34:18

I've found that there are always two sides to every story."

"No, I can't agree with you there, Pastor," the man said, shaking his head slowly from side to side. "You can live as straight as you want to live, and that doesn't mean your spouse is going to do the same."

The lights finally came on in my slow-moving brain, and I realized my conversation partner was talking about himself. I'd made my comment in reference to divorce, voicing the idea that both parties usually bear some of the responsibility for the breakdown of a marriage. My friend disagreed, and at last I understood why. His wife had deserted him years ago. After a few years of marriage, she concluded that the quiet life of a small-town shopkeeper was not for her. In what sounds like the refrain from a country song, she left him with a business to run, a mortgage to pay, and two little girls to raise on his own. Though this man had been remarried for decades now, our brief exchange revealed that his resentment over that betrayal was still fresh. The wound of rejection is slow to heal.

The stereotype in our society is that men are abusers, sexually unfaithful, betrayers of their families. That is true of some. Yet many men, too, are victims of infidelity. According to one study, 19 percent of women admit to having had an extramarital affair (21 percent for men), which means that nearly one in five husbands have experienced the heartbreak of infidelity.[2]

The same stereotype that pictures men as abusers complicates their position as victims. Indeed, many are reluctant to admit that they have "been cheated on," fearing a loss of esteem among their peers. They bury the pain of rejection, unwilling to let others see that they feel unloved. Others react with anger, even violence, as if shouting, threatening, or punching through walls will dull the pain. In either case, the heart cries with desperate questions: "Why doesn't she love me?" "What's wrong with me?" "If my own wife doesn't want me, who would?"

Would you believe that God also knows the pain of being unloved? Through the prophets, God often used the metaphor of a jilted husband to depict His relationship with His people. In the most famous, and graphic, example, the prophet Hosea married a woman who had multiple affairs, and he kept taking her back to demonstrate that God loves His people despite their unfaithfulness. If anyone understands what it feels like to be rejected by a loved one, God does. And He continues to love us just the same.

God's love for you is strong, permanent, and never conditional. He does not love you only if you are the ideal partner, only if you live up to His expectations, only if you are interesting or virile or successful. He just loves you.

No human experience compares to this profound love. Parental love comes closest, perhaps, but even that falls short of the perfect love that God has for you. God loves you when you deserve it, and when you don't. He loves you when you're at your athletic best, and at your paunchy worst. He loves you when you bring home that killer commission, and when you lose your job. God loves you when you're witty, debonair, and stylish, and when you're a klutz. He loves you when you're James Bond, and Mickey Mouse, and anybody in between. God loves you even when others don't. And that's a promise that will never be broken.

A TIMELY TIP

Love people, but put your
full trust only in God.

LAWRENCE WELK

TRY IT

Tell someone that you love them today.

A PRAYER

Lord, I don't feel loved sometimes, or loveable.
I'm sometimes angry at the people who I thought
would love me but don't, and I'm so grateful
for Your unwavering acceptance.
Thank You for loving me, and help me to be
as loving toward others as You are to me.
Amen.

DAY 9

WELCOME
ACCOUNTABILITY

THE PROMISE

You can be free from sinful habits.

No temptation has overtaken you except
what is common to mankind. And God is faithful;
he will not let you be tempted beyond what you can bear.
But when you are tempted, he will also provide
a way out so that you can endure it.

1 CORINTHIANS 10:13

Addiction. Somebody had to say it. In these days, that's something Christian men need to talk about. Too often we don't. Even at church. But addictive substances and practices are all around us. Porn is always available—on the computer, on the phone, on cable TV, just a click away. It's available. And enticing. Alcohol is nearly as available and even more socially acceptable. Few people notice another's drinking habits, and they're easily concealed. Narcotics, gambling, and other habits can be equally entrapping. While most men are not addicts, some are, and some others are dependent on substances or behaviors in an unhealthy way. They struggle with bad habits they just can't break. Chances are good that someone you know wrestles with a problem behavior or substance, which may go unnoticed or be casually explained away.

It's embarrassing. Many men carry the secret burden of a behavior that damages both family and soul. For some Christian men, habits involving pornography, gambling, alcohol, or other harmful behaviors have become the one thing they cannot control. They may be great dads, sensitive husbands, hard workers, excellent providers, tithers, Little League coaches, and Sunday school teachers. They may have a master's degree, a corner office, and 5 percent body fat, yet they are helpless to the allure of sexual images or "just one more" drink or an adrenaline high.

If that describes you or someone you know, it may help to know that you're not alone. My friend Jerry is a pastor in Pennsylvania. He said, "Over the years, many men have asked—even begged—for prayer and help in this area. I think of the confession, with tears, of one of our dear saints on his deathbed. He was desperate for freedom." Being born again does not provide a force field that keeps unwholesome thoughts from entering your brain or harmful substances from affecting your body. Christian men struggle with these things too.

And that's a key word, *struggle*. In the case of pornography, only a small minority of users report feeling much guilt about it. The fact that a man does feel guilt over secret harmful behavior is a positive thing. It shows that the Spirit is at work in the heart, revealing the harm it can do to him and others, making them want to quit. That sense of conviction is God's way of moving us out of the darkness and into the light. Embracing that struggle is a positive step.

And here is God's promise: you can overcome addiction. The attraction to an addictive substance or practice, like any temptation, can seem overwhelming. It can grip your mind, raise your blood pressure, make your heart pound, and drive you to action. But it is not irresistible.

Another friend, Richard, is a pastor who kept his porn addiction secret for many years. Finally, in desperation, he reached out for help. He found a mentor who had gained victory after a similar struggle. Richard started on the road to recovery, confessing his powerlessness and asking God for deliverance. He joined a support group. He confessed to his wife, then to his congregation. He spent hours in prayer and months learning new ways of thinking and behaving. And he has been "sober," as he thinks of it, for more than four years. Others have found victory over addiction, and you will too.

For most people, overcoming this practice takes a bit of time and includes a good deal of prayer and accountability. I don't know how your journey will unfold, but I know how it will begin: with two baby steps. One is to tell God about your problem, and the other is to tell someone else. That is the start of your walk to freedom, and it's just two small steps away. You can do this, with the Spirit's help. I know you can. I'll be praying for you.

A TIMELY TIP

Nothing paralyzes our lives like the attitude
that things can never change.
We need to remind ourselves
that God can change things.

WARREN WIERSBE

TRY IT

Share your struggle with someone you trust,
and ask for his prayer and guidance
in seeking victory.

THE PRAYER

Lord, I am tired of carrying this secret.
I'm tired of the struggle, and the guilt and shame.
I long to be free. I confess my need to You.
Guide me in the path to freedom.
Amen.

DAY 10

BE A PEACE MAKER

THE PROMISE

You can win more battles
by talking than by fighting.

Blessed are the peacemakers,
for they will be called children of God.

MATTHEW 5:9

What would a reasonable man do? That's the question." My lawyer friend was explaining the legal
standard in a liability case he was defending. The plaintiff
charged that his client had been negligent in tending his
responsibility, leading to a loss of property through a fire.

"What do you have to do to win?" I'd asked my friend.
He explained that the standard was simple—and not so
simple. He had to show that his client had done what any
reasonable person would have done in his place.

But where is this "reasonable man"? These days he's
become harder to find than a buffalo nickel. It seems that
we live in an age of unreasonableness. People seldom operate
based on facts, logic, or reason. Instead, everyone seems
driven by some form of tribalism or outrage. Public debates
have become shouting matches in which each contestant
vies to outinsult the other. It seems that everyone in the
public square reduces complicated arguments to memorable

sound bites, then drops the mic and walks away. The rancor in our discourse, the constant finger pointing and belittling, have many of us wondering whatever became of that reasonable man.

In this climate, many men feel anger that borders on rage. Others feel horror or disgust. Some feel a deep sense of powerlessness or insignificance. Many simply want to withdraw, believing that the regular guy, the person who sees both sides of an argument and wants to promote harmony, has no role to play. The world belongs to those who can "demolish" their opponents, "destroy" their arguments, and "pound" sense into their heads.

In this context, Christian men face three options. We can fight anger with more anger, pouring gasoline on the public outrage that has swept our society in hopes of somehow advancing the gospel. Or we can withdraw from the world, battening down the hatches on our lifeboat and pretending that the screaming outside has nothing to do with us. Or we can be peacemakers.

We are not the first generation to inhabit a culture in which ridicule replaced discussion. The world Jesus entered was ruled by tyrants, riddled with corruption, and riven by conflict. Terrorism? Check. Suppression of dissent? Check. Political scandal? Check. The first century had it all. And to His followers—men and women accustomed to the identity politics of Jew versus Gentile, slave versus free, male versus female—Jesus taught a better way. Blessed, or happy, are those who are humble, selfless, and merciful. Blessed are the reconcilers, the moderators, those who go the extra mile. Blessed are those who make peace with others, for they will be called the children of God.

Peacemaking is risky business. Those who attempt it are sometimes called soft, weak, or some other effete name. Or they may be labeled a loser, bigot, or hater. Our culture loves to name call. Yet it may be worth that risk in order to wear the one nametag that really matters: child of God. Is there a place in today's world for the reasonable man? There most certainly is. And I pray that you will be that man.

A TIMELY TIP

Darkness cannot drive out darkness;
only light can do that.
Hate cannot drive out hate,
only love can do that.
MARTIN LUTHER KING JR.

TRY IT

Today, engage in conversation
with someone with whom you disagree,
but rather than give opinions,
simply listen and ask questions.

A PRAYER

"God, grant me the serenity to accept
the things I cannot change,
courage to change the things I can,
and wisdom to know the difference.
Amen." [3]

DAY 11

— — —

BE CONTENT

THE PROMISE

The satisfaction you seek
is found in God.

Life does not consist in an abundance of possessions.

For me it was Hot Wheels cars. I got a GTO and a woodie station wagon along with a few feet of plastic track for Christmas. Dad and I set up a dragstrip, complete with a loop-the-loop, on the hardwood floor in the hallway. I was hooked. I think Dad was too, because he went out the next day and bought two more cars and a jump. We played with those cars for hours, tweaking the wire axles to get the wheels aligned just right. Dad even tried some silicone spray on the track. Anything to increase velocity.

Those were great times, but they sparked something deadly within me, besides the need for speed. Hot Wheels kindled my desire for more. From then on I was saving my allowance and begging to do extra chores so I could buy just one more car. And another, and another. A few years later I watched my own kids feed that same craving with Pokémon cards and American Girl dolls. And I graduated from die-cast models to books and tools, each purchased with the promise that it would be the last. All I needed was *one* more.

For some guys it's one more dollar. For others, one more

stroke off the handicap, or one more power tool in the garage, or one more car or bike or electronic gadget. We might substitute the words *bigger*, *better*, or *latest* in place of more. The idea is constant: what we have is not quite enough. This next acquisition will scratch the deep-down itch for satisfaction or completion.

Jesus told a story about a guy who always wanted one more. You can read it in Luke 12:13–21. It's about a man who had a knack for making money. In those days, that meant producing a good crop, and he did so in abundance. *I just need a little bit more,* the fellow thought. *Just a little more grain in the stockpile, and just one more barn to hold it. Then I'll be set for life.* Sadly, God interrupted this daydream of consumer revelry with a shocking pronouncement: "You fool! This very night your life will be demanded from you. Then who will get what you have prepared for yourself?" (verse 20).

That's a great question. What will be the value of having one more, or the best, or the latest, or the biggest when your life comes to an end? That moment may be the first when some men see the true worth of the things they've spent their lives pursuing: nothing.

We acquire things in an effort to find value in our lives. We're really trying to say, "See, my life amounts to something after all." And it does. But the significance we seek cannot be found in a pile of toys, no matter how expensive they are or how fast they go. Genuine satisfaction comes from being right on the inside, doing right, feeling good about who you are, being in satisfying relationships. Those things cannot be had at Walmart—or Cabela's. They come from being in a right relationship with God, learning to discern His voice, doing what's right even when it's difficult, caring more about other people than about ourselves, and, sometimes, from setting toys aside in order to focus on the things that really matter. The good news? Those are all things you can do.

I don't know what became of my Hot Wheels collection. The last time I saw the GTO, it was all banged up and missing two wheels. I smashed it with a hammer just to see what would happen. Things don't last, and they never satisfy the true desires of the heart. My family, on the other hand, is still a source of unbelievable joy. Since I was ten years old, my relationship with God has grown considerably. The things that make life worthwhile are real, and chances are good that they're already in your life. They just can't be parked in a garage.

A TIMELY TIP

If everyone demanded peace
instead of another television set,
then there'd be peace.

JOHN LENNON

TRY IT

Identify the ten material possessions
that you value most,
then give one of them away.

A PRAYER

---

*Lord, I crave things more than I crave
spending time with You. I often place more value
on my stuff than on the people around me.
Plant a hunger in my soul for the things
that truly matter. Help me to love You
and love others more than
any of the things You have given me.
Amen.*

DAY 12
— — —

BUILD
RELATIONSHIPS

THE PROMISE

God will never leave you,
even when you feel most alone.

There is a friend who sticks closer than a brother.

PROVERBS 18:24

Many men, both single and married, are intensely lonely. We think of marriage as a defense against loneliness. Some naïvely believe that the other side of the altar is a Promised Land of companionship and nonstop affection. Many are surprised and disappointed to find that marriage does not cure all existential ills. Like all relationships, it brings its own challenges as well as rewards.

One reason for loneliness is that some lack a context for building affirming relationships. Being single can lead to a certain level of social exclusion as couples socialize with couples. Some married men find little companionship with their spouses. Though they share a home, a family, and are bonded together, they may communicate little about matters of the heart. They may keep workplace relationships shallow, have few or no close friends, and wonder how they came to feel so alone while surrounded by people. One more night in front of the television, another weekend working on the house, and suddenly life seems solitary.

Into this haze of aloneness, Jesus shines a ray of hope and

companionship. He promises rest for the weary soul and a friendship that supersedes any human company. "God has said, 'Never will I leave you; never will I forsake you.' So we say with confidence, 'The Lord is my helper'" (Hebrews 13:5–6). There is a friend who sticks closer than a brother. When you feel the acute lack of human intimacy, know that God is with you. He loves you and cares about you, even when it seems that no one else does. Through the presence of the Holy Spirit, you are never truly alone.

And there is hope for the married lonely. In an ironic twist, we often find that those who feel the least secure and hungry for companionship find that it eludes them, while those who are self-confident and adventuresome may attract attention without trying. When you do not expect your wife to provide every ounce of the relational connection that you need, she may feel a freedom that sparks new interest in your companionship. Friendships, interests, hobbies, sports, or community involvement will enrich your life, break your boredom, and, who knows, may cause your partner to look at you with fresh eyes. The surest way to have a friend is to be one, so the saying goes. And the surest way to find companionship with your spouse is to be a person who is secure, engaged, and interesting enough to attract her attention.

"Do you ever get lonely, living by yourself?" I asked my friend Daniel.

"No," he answered without hesitation. Fortysomething and never married, Daniel's life was packed with satisfying relationships: respected colleagues at work, cherished members of a small group at church, and long-term friendships. Then Daniel paused. "Let me qualify that," he said. "When I am connected with people in meaningful ways, I never feel alone. In fact, I crave alone time. When I let those connections slip away, then yes, I sometimes feel lonely."

Know that you are loved by God and treasure His presence. Build the relationships you have into strong, nurturing friendships. It'll do your soul good.

A TIMELY TIP

Friendship is one of the sweetest joys of life.
Many might have failed beneath the bitterness
of their trial had they not found a friend.

CHARLES H. SPURGEON

TRY IT

Sometime this month, tackle an item
on your bucket list, and invite someone
you love to come along.

A PRAYER

Lord, I bring my loneliness to You.
You know my heart and my need.
Grant me the gift of peace and contentment, I pray.
Through Your Holy Spirit, be present with me.
And give me opportunities to connect with others.
Amen.

DAY 13

HAVE HOPE

You're going to grow stronger.

He who began a good work in you will carry it on
to completion until the day of Christ Jesus.
PHILIPPIANS 1:6

T here's a . . . Mark here to see you?" The receptionist
sounded quizzical because Mark wasn't a vendor or
client. He was a friend, dropping by the office for an unexpected midday visit.

"Sure, send him up," I said, then stepped into the hallway
to greet my pal. Once seated in my office, he asked if we
could close the door. Now I was feeling quizzical. "What's
up?" I asked, trying not to sound too surprised to see him.

Mark stretched his neck backward, looking at the ceiling,
and passed a hand over his tightened brow. "I screwed up,
man. Big time. Lisa's telling me to grow up or get out. I don't
know if there's any coming back from this one."

I sat for a long minute pondering Mark's painful
situation and realizing how easily some combination of
selfishness and stupidity can bring any man to the same
place. The realization that you have disappointed the people
you love brings a horrible, hollow feeling. Mark's issue was
gambling. The issue may be different for other men, but

the feeling of frustration and stupidity over selfish mistakes remains constant. Disappointing others produces a cascade of emotions that lands on two burning questions: "How could I have been such an idiot?" and "What do I do now?"

That pain is doubled in the case of repeated failure. With each fall off the wagon, the disappointment piles higher and the questions grow more urgent. *Is there any coming back from this? Can my family forgive me? Is change possible? Will I ever break free from these self-destructive patterns?*

For Mark, the answer to all those questions was yes. Change began for him on the day he found the courage to tell one friend about his situation and ask for help. His road was a long one, as it is for every man breaking long-term strongholds and rebuilding trust. Yet Mark made it. He and Lisa reconciled, continued raising their teen daughter, and are now proud in-laws and grandparents. All of that was made possible by his willingness to trust this basic tenet of the gospel: your past does not have to be repeated in the future. With God's help, you can be stronger tomorrow than you are today.

Many men give up on the future because they're so burdened by the past that they can see no hope. Frankly, the people who love them sometimes give up too. The wounds caused by selfish behaviors can make reconciliation difficult. Regardless, there is hope for the future. As a believer in Jesus Christ, you have invited the power of the Holy Spirit into your life. The changes you have been unable to make, He can make in you. The courage and discipline that have eluded you can be found. Self-indulgent behaviors can be broken. The day you hit rock bottom is the first day you begin to climb, and here is God's promise to you: He will not stop transforming your life until you are *completely* made new.

"I'm sorry, brother," I said to Mark. "I feel for you. And I love you. I know God has got something better in store. He's not finished with you yet."

And that's exactly what I say to you.

A TIMELY TIP

When we pray for the Spirit's help . . .
we will simply fall down
at the Lord's feet in our weakness.
There we will find the victory and power
that comes from His love.

ANDREW MURRAY

TRY IT

Invite a trusted friend to hold you
accountable and pray for you concerning
your area of greatest weakness.

A PRAYER

Lord, I screwed up. I'm disappointed in myself,
and I know my family is disappointed in me too.
The one thing I'm clinging to
is that I know You love me. Please help.
Give me hope for the future.
Amen.

DAY 14

DARE TO FORGIVE

THE PROMISE

Grace is a gift
you'll never regret giving.

> *Blessed are the merciful,*
> *for they will be shown mercy.*
> MATTHEW 5:7

I have a question about forgiveness. It regards a situation where my wife has been not exactly faithful while I'm in here. How do I handle that?"

I was accompanying friends who were teaching prison inmates on topics including anger, joy, grace, and forgiveness. After a session of biblical and practical instruction, the speaker opened the floor for questions. "Ask anything," he said. One man's hand shot into the air, and the question burning in his mind was anything but hypothetical. How is it possible to forgive a spouse who has been unfaithful? Can anyone overcome that kind of betrayal? Should they? Fifty men leaned in to hear the answer.

Unforgiveness is a bitter poison for any who hold it. It withers the soul, wringing out the last drops of grace and joy, leaving a withered husk in their place. Anger and resentment are thieves that rob you of sleep, joy, and contentment. They are con men, enticing you to trade your peace of mind for the satisfaction of revenge, a reward you will never realize.

The first reason to forgive is to free yourself from the prison of bitterness that will surely destroy your soul if you let it.

Yet forgiveness and reconciliation are two different things. To forgive is to surrender the right (and need) for revenge. To forgive is to hand one's anger over to God, as the apostle Paul advises: "Do not take revenge, my dear friends, but leave room for God's wrath, for it is written: 'It is mine to avenge; I will repay,' says the Lord" (Romans 12:19). It is possible to forgive anyone. To be reconciled, however, is something more. It is to be brought back into full relationship with the offender. That will involve godly sorrow, possibly restitution, and the penance of time. All of that is impossible with someone who is unrepentant, unremorseful, or refuses to take responsibility for their actions. Sadly, reconciliation is not always possible, even when we are willing to forgive.

In the end, it is God who grants us the grace to forgive others. My friend responded to the inmate's question by relating the story of Corrie ten Boom, a survivor of a Nazi concentration camp who became a noted evangelist. One day after speaking on the subject of forgiveness, a man approached Corrie. She recognized him as one of her former captors, a guard at the Ravensbrück camp, though he did not recognize her. He said, "I have become a Christian. I know that God has forgiven me for the cruel things I did [at Ravensbrück], but I would like to hear it from your lips as well. Fräulein . . . will you forgive me?"

In that instant, Corrie ten Boom was forced to answer that pressing question: *Is it possible to forgive, and if so, should I?* She later wrote,

> It could not have been many seconds that he stood there, hand held out, but to me it seemed hours as I wrestled with the most difficult thing I had ever had to do. . . . I knew it not only as a commandment of God, but as a daily experience. Since the end of the war I had had a home in Holland for victims of Nazi brutality. Those who were able to forgive their former enemies were able also to return to the outside world and rebuild their lives, no matter what the physical scars. Those who nursed their bitterness remained invalids. It was as simple and as horrible as that.

Finally, she breathed this silent prayer: "Jesus, help me! . . . I can lift my hand. I can do that much. You supply the feeling." She later wrote, "And then this healing warmth seemed to flood my whole being, bringing tears to my eyes. 'I forgive you, brother!' I cried. 'With all my heart!'"[4]

Yes, it is possible to forgive. Yes, you, too, can do it. Grace is the one gift you will never regret giving.

A TIMELY TIP

Forgiveness is the key that unlocks the door
of resentment and the handcuffs of hate.

CORRIE TEN BOOM

TRY IT

Imagine a future in which both you
and your enemy are able to lead happy
and productive lives.

A PRAYER

Lord, I have carried bitterness in my heart
for so long that it seems a part of me.
I have wanted the one who hurt me to suffer
as I have suffered. I have longed for revenge.
Take this burden from me.
Set me free by Your grace. Help me to forgive.
Amen.

DAY 15

BE ENCOURAGED

THE PROMISE

Hang in there, and you will make it.

Let us not become weary in doing good,
for at the proper time we will reap a harvest
if we do not give up.

Jesus said, "Blessed are the meek," but the world now seems to belong to the loudmouths. Social media could be called "social hysteria" because it's riddled with screeching. Religion, politics, parenting—everyone seems to have an opinion, and the most obnoxious voices go viral, garnering far more attention than they're worth. Reasonable, thoughtful people command little attention and even less chance of being heard. It can be infuriating.

Work can be no less a frustration as it seems the laziest or most unscrupulous employees are not only tolerated but sometimes promoted ahead of the honest worker. You show up on time, work hard, produce solid results, don't fudge the numbers, but where's the reward? The guy who fibs on the expense report and spends the afternoon playing solitaire always gets the bonus. Is that fair?

What isn't fair is donating to the church and giving something to the local food bank while watching the neighbors spend every dime they earn (and a few more they've borrowed) on themselves. They take four kids to Disney World every summer, while the generous giver takes another lap on the mower.

All of this makes one wonder if there's any point in living a righteous life. Where's the profit in working hard, filing your taxes, paying your bills, and telling the truth when the people who manipulate the system seem to be running the world?

That's an excellent question, so good in fact that it's one of the few that the Bible addresses directly. Listen to the way a writer named Asaph put it:

> For I envied the arrogant
> when I saw the prosperity of the wicked.
> They have no struggles;
> their bodies are healthy and strong.
> They are free from common human burdens;
> they are not plagued by human ills.
> Therefore pride is their necklace;
> they clothe themselves with violence.
> . . . .
> This is what the wicked are like—
> always free of care, they go on amassing wealth.
> Surely in vain I have kept my heart pure
> and have washed my hands in innocence. (Psalm 73:2–6,
>   12–13)

We don't know who Asaph was, but he's singing our song. It often seems more profitable to bend the rules or even break them than to be a good guy and do what you're supposed to do. It makes you feel like a chump.

You're not. When you live decently, honestly, fairly, in obedience to the ways of God, you're anything but a chump. In fact, it is the "wicked" who have everything to lose. Asaph writes further, about the realization that comes to him, "When I tried to understand all this, it troubled me deeply till I entered the sanctuary of God; then I understood their final destiny. Surely you place them on slippery ground; you cast them down to ruin. How suddenly are they destroyed, completely swept away by terrors!" (Psalm 73:16–19).

Arrogant, dishonest people may seem to have life by the tail, but they don't. By defying God, they're skating on thin ice, according to the psalm writer. Any day now they'll plunge into the icy water of financial ruin, or public ridicule, or abandonment by their family, or even criminal prosecution. And if by chance they escape those consequences in this life, they have estranged themselves from God, which is a far greater punishment. When did the lights come on for Asaph? When he caught a glimpse of the holiness, goodness, and power of God.

Focus on who God is, and do not compare yourself to others, especially those who don't know Him. Keep on loving God and loving others. You will be rewarded at the proper time.

A TIMELY TIP

Virtue is its own reward, and brings with it
the truest and highest pleasure.

JOHN HENRY NEWMAN

TRY IT

Name three good reasons to do
the right thing, even when
you don't have to,
then share that thought with a friend.

A PREYER

A PRAYER

*Lord, sometimes I wonder what's the use.
I try to do what's right and keep a good attitude,
but it's lonely out here. Give me just a glimpse
of Yourself today. Remind me of the glory
that You have in store.
Amen.*

DAY 16

WELCOME OTHERS

THE PROMISE

Other people bring a blessing to your life.

Y ou have *got* to be kidding me." I couldn't believe my wife would even ask that, knowing how much I treasure privacy.

"It's only for a week, maybe less."

"But we don't even know the guy."

"What's to know? He's from Egypt, coming to America to study. It'll be fun. And interesting."

My wife and I have different temperaments, which produce different views on hospitality. She would love for our home to be a hostel for travelers, students, people in transition, stray cats—basically anyone without a place to live. Me? I like a little space.

In this case, she was asking about hosting an international student arriving to study at a nearby university. The graduate studies office had asked if anyone could provide temporary accommodations while he secured housing and transportation.

"Whatever," I said without enthusiasm. "It's only for a week though, right?"

Ahmad was cheerful enough when he arrived from Cairo. And on the drive home from the airport, I was determined to make the best of it. "What are you studying?" I asked.

"English literature. I'm working on a doctorate."

"And your family, what line of work are they in?"

"My father is an imam."

"You mean like a Muslim cleric?"

"Precisely. And what do you do?"

"I'm a pastor," I said, trying not to look in the rearview mirror. I shot a glance at my spouse, and I'm sure she knew what I was thinking: *What did you get me into?*

For some men, other people are like a stone in the shoe, an irritant to be endured as briefly as possible. They come into your life from unexpected angles—at work, in social settings, or family gatherings. They bring with them annoying habits, ridiculous opinions, wrong-headed religious and political views. They cost you money or time or convenience. Though you might not put it this strongly, many men would agree with Jean-Paul Sartre that "hell is—other people." All in all, life would be better if everybody stayed in their own lane.

That's one way of looking at the presence of others in our lives. Scripture offers a better view. Other people provide us with love and companionship, with advice and encouragement, with correction and learning. They open our minds and open our hearts. Welcoming other people expands our world so that we are changed for the better. When we show hospitality by welcoming people into conversations, into our churches and small groups, onto our teams, at our tables, and, yes, into our homes, it makes our lives infinitely richer. Other people bring a blessing to our lives.

It's true that some people are boorish and ill-mannered. Some are takers, abusers. We must be aware of the potential for danger when bringing ourselves into contact with others. But those dangers mustn't prevent us from experiencing the great joy of hospitality.

When we arrived home from the airport, Ahmad presented us with hospitality gifts, a delightful custom in his culture. We shared many meals together, And he was eager to cook for us, introducing us to what have become favorite foods. We held long conversations about geopolitics and education and even religion. When the week was up, we parted with a warm embrace and the knowledge that a friendship had begun, one that continues to this day.

"You were right," I said to my wife. "That was a really good thing to do."

"I know," she said, and gave me a little peck on the cheek. "You're learning."

A TIMELY TIP

Whenever we develop significant friendships
with those who are not like us culturally,
we become broader, wiser persons.

RICHARD J. FOSTER

TRY IT

Invite someone who is not
a close friend to coffee, and listen.

A PRAYER

Lord, I want to be open to others,
but I'm afraid of losing out. I cherish my time
and my personal space. Bring me opportunities
to be open and generous with others,
and give me the wisdom and patience to take them.
Amen.

DAY 17

– – –

GIVE GENEROUSLY

THE PROMISE

You gain by giving.

The one who blesses others is abundantly blessed;
those who help others are helped.

PROVERBS 11:25 MSG

Sometimes it seems as though everybody wants something from you. It starts, for some, when a wife or roommate moves in and takes over half the apartment—or more. A buddy at work asks for help moving, and there goes a perfectly good Saturday. Somebody is collecting for the United Way. That's twenty bucks out of your wallet. And whatever your occupation—bricklayer or lawyer, web designer or plumber—everyone you know will eventually hit you up for free advice. Your time, your money, and even your home all seem to be up for grabs. Sometimes you feel like snarling at the world, "You want a piece of me? Do ya?" but you don't dare. Most of the people you know would say, "Sure, I'll take fifty bucks or an hour's labor. Your choice."

Feeling put upon or taken advantage of creates a dark space inside your head. In that black hole, negative thoughts like resentment and entitlement can take root. Before long, you may feel irritated at family members for, well, existing, or exasperated with coworkers for, surprise, being imperfect, or annoyed with neighbors or church leaders for requesting one more slice of your time.

If that sounds familiar, here's a warning: feelings of resentment and entitlement are salted earth that brings forth poisonous fruit in your life. Anger, sexual sin, even violence can grow from the dangerous thought that "I have a right to be happy, and it's my turn now."

Sure, there's a legitimate line between being a pal and being a patsy. Self-care, guarding your time and energy, managing your money well—all of those are important concerns. Yet one of the delightful discoveries of growing in Christ is the realization that other people add much more to your life than they take. Ironically, that becomes most evident when you give to them rather than receiving from them. Sharing, giving, being generous, helping others, doing favors, lending a hand even when it costs you something—these are not burdensome duties but opportunities to be blessed. When we give ourselves with a willing heart, we gain much more in return.

Still, it can take a mental adjustment to adopt an attitude of openness to others. It helps to realize that this is one of those spiritual principles that is highly practical advice. Generosity is not an ascetic duty designed to produce holiness through suffering. When you give to others, you receive something good in return. Both are blessed in the transaction.

Some call this karma. Others describe the phenomenon with the glib phrase "What goes around comes around." Both are attempts to describe the principle that Jesus declared with the simple statement, "Give, and it will be given to you. A good measure, pressed down, shaken together and running over, will be poured into your lap. For with the measure you use, it will be measured to you" (Luke 6:38). It's not a simple quid pro quo, but there is a true exchange of value between giver and receiver.

This works in reverse too. Jesus also taught, "Do not judge, or you too will be judged. For in the same way you judge others, you will be judged, and with the measure you use, it will be measured to you" (Matthew 7:1–2). Those who offer a closed fist to the world will find that they receive little in return. Like the law of gravity, this principle simply describes the way the world works. Generous people are blessed in relationships, and selfish people encounter problems with people.

Resolve to be a giver, not a taker. Practice the art of generosity, and you'll find that you have all you need, including friends, in abundance. Try it and see.

A TIMELY TIP

When you focus on being a blessing,
God makes sure that you
are always blessed in abundance.

JOEL OSTEEN

TRY IT

Be on the lookout
for someone to help today.

A PRAYER

Lord, sometimes I get tired of being the one everybody counts on. I give a lot. Sometimes it feels unfair. Help me see beyond my weariness to the joy of helping others. Make me a blessing. Amen.

DAY 18

BE YOURSELF

THE PROMISE

You are good for something.

*Now to each one the manifestation of the Spirit is given
for the common good. . . . All these are the work
of one and the same Spirit, and he distributes them
to each one, just as he determines.*

1 CORINTHIANS 12:7, 11

I served as a pastor for two decades, and the low point of nearly every year was our annual clergy gathering. On the one hand, it was a chance to see pastors from around the region with whom I had little contact, a kind of reunion. But that relational boost was more than counterbalanced by the negative emotions that rose from comparing the results of our work. Every year, statistical reports were published showing the numerical and financial progress of each congregation. Awards were given to the most successful pastors, which meant that a half-dozen or so received a commendation while seventy-five others seethed with envy. That sounds terribly unspiritual, I know. But ministers are human too. It was frustrating to realize that, despite a year of hard work and sacrifice, others had won more souls, preached better sermons, raised more money, or built a bigger church. It is exhausting to compare oneself to others in terms of ministry achievement.

The problem of achievement envy goes way, way back in the history of the church, and it's not limited to members of the clergy. Some church members also cast a jealous eye toward other congregations, especially those that seem to be growing the fastest, and direct that same critical glance toward one another. That was certainly true of the earliest Christians, who immediately fell into the sin of comparison. I don't mean only those in Corinth, to whom Paul wrote specifically about this problem. The apostles themselves had more than one squabble about who was the most spiritual, most accomplished, closest to Jesus. It's bad enough to succumb to that jealous bickering at a church board meeting or a potluck. Imagine arguing about it in front of Jesus Himself. We do that too, of course, because Jesus is present wherever two or three of us are gathered—feeding the hungry, defending orphans and widows, swapping stories about who had the largest crowd on Easter.

The apostle Paul made two points to remember about spiritual abilities. One is that they are gifts, meaning they're not something we create on our own. We have them only because they were given to us by God. So even if you have a legit superpower (yes, that's one of the gifts, called "miraculous powers" in 1 Corinthians 12:10), that means only that *you* can't perform miracles. It's something God does through you, despite your limitations. The same is true for all spiritual gifts, including preaching, evangelism, and leadership.

A second thing to remember is that gifts are distributed individually and not everybody gets the same one. In this sense, they're like eye color or height. You have no choice in the matter; you get what God gives you, and it'll be different from the guy next to you. So there's no use comparing your spiritual gifts or achievements to anyone else's. Sure, it's fine to notice that you have brown eyes and the other guy's are blue. But so what? It's not like either of you had anything to say about it. You may be gifted with generosity or service or healing while someone else is given the ability to teach or lead. Big deal. The point is that everybody is good for something, and each person should concentrate on doing what God has given *him* to do.

One year at the annual clergy gathering, I heard my name called for the Excellence in Ministry Award. I would have acted surprised, but I knew it was coming. The criteria for the award were well known, and I had realized weeks before that I would qualify. I took my place on the podium along with a few other pastors, and we each received a certificate and a pat on the back, then everybody applauded. And you know what I felt? Nothing. It turns out that receiving the praise for what God has accomplished isn't all that satisfying. Rather than envying the work of others, it's better just to be yourself. God made you as a unique person, endowed you with gifts, and turned you loose in the world. Be the person God made you to be. That's the one thing no one else can do!

A TIMELY TIP

We love one another, serve one another,
help one another, and in so doing
we see how God has equipped us to do so.
RUSSELL D. MOORE

TRY IT

Ask two close friends what unique abilities
they see in you, then ask God
for opportunities to use those gifts.

A PRAYER

Lord, I know it's not right to be jealous,
but sometimes I am. When I compare myself
to someone who seems more gifted or mature,
I feel like a dunce. Jesus, help me to be more like me,
the person You have called and gifted me to be.
Amen.

DAY 19

— — —

TALK WITH GOD

THE PROMISE

God will meet you wherever you are.

Show me your ways, LORD,
teach me your paths.
PSALM 25:4

In my seminary days, I had a professor who was both pietistic and bombastic. That's an odd combination, yet he was a wonderful teacher and greatly respected by his students. On some mornings—he seemed to prefer eight o'clock classes—he would begin class by singing a hymn. A capella. In full voice. Without so much as a howdy do, he'd start belting, "A mighty fortress is our God! A bulwark never failing!" Students would dutifully stand and croak out a few bars, producing more phlegm than harmony.

On other days, this delightful, quixotic man would begin class by asking, "So what did you get from your quiet time this morning?" Then he would pause, for a long time, waiting for an answer while three dozen students avoided eye contact. Prof was an early riser and communed with the Father before daybreak. By class time, he had already reflected on Scripture, talked with the Lord, drawn a spiritual lesson for the day, and probably graded a few papers. Most of us were happy to be both present and awake at 8:00 a.m. If our teacher began the day with a spiritual victory, ours was launched in defeat, feeling useless because we had not had "daily devotions" before heading off to school.

Many Christians hold an unstated expectation that everyone should begin each day with prayer and Bible reading. Without doubt, this practice of morning devotions is a treasured discipline for many folk. Advocates of the practice have a good deal of biblical and historical support. After all, Jesus often snuck away from the crowds, possibly every day, for prayer (Luke 5:16), and the great reformer Martin Luther reportedly said, "I have so much to do that I shall spend the first three hours in prayer." *Three hours!* You may know someone who lives by this daily routine of prayer and Scripture reading, or you may do yourself.

But not everyone does, and, I'm convinced, not everyone should. The reason is not because daily prayer and Bible reading are pointless. Far from it. But they are only *one* type of spiritual practice that can enrich our relationship with God, and one size simply doesn't fit all. There are far too many spiritual practices to insist that every man on earth adopt just this one.

In nearly every other aspect of life, we understand and accept the temperamental differences among people. Teachers know that not all students learn in the same way. Some learn by hearing, some by watching, and some by doing. Employers know that not all workers have the same strengths. Some are strategic thinkers, others are doers. Some thrive on meeting new challenges each day, others perform best in what may seem to be a monotonous routine.

A similar principle holds true in spiritual practices. Some people crave the predictable routine of beginning each day with a brief time of prayer and Bible reading. Others prefer more intensive times of prayer, as Luther did. Some read the Bible for ten minutes a day. Others study it for an extended block of time every week or two. A few will memorize a single verse and meditate on it for days or more at a stretch. Some prefer silence, meditation, and private prayer, while others thrive on communal practices like worship, study, and corporate prayer. What matters most is not *how* we connect with God but *that* we do. Of the dozen or so classic spiritual practices—including prayer, Scripture, meditation, fasting, solitude, worship, silence, and service—one or two will be especially helpful in bringing you into communion with God. Developing your own spiritual rhythm will produce far better results than copying someone else's.

I think of my old professor and his loud singing now and then. Sometimes I wonder how he'll react when he moves on to his eternal reward and encounters, like the apostle John, "silence in heaven for about half an hour" (Revelation 8:1). I think he'll fare about as well as a first-year divinity student trying to hit high C first before breakfast. But when they shout "Hallelujah!" I'm sure his will be the loudest voice. We each worship God in our own way.

A TIMELY TIP

[God] created you with a certain personality
and a certain spiritual temperament.
God wants your worship,
according to the way He made you.
GARY L. THOMAS

TRY IT

Choose a spiritual practice that's less familiar
to you, like fasting, silence, solitude,
or service, and give it a try.

A PRAYER

*Lord, I want to experience Your presence,
but I'm not sure how. When I imitate
what others do, it feels forced.
Help me understand how my heart connects
with You, and lead me to do that often.
Amen.*

DAY 20

- - -

MAKE FRIENDS

THE PROMISE

Friendships will enrich your life.

As iron sharpens iron,
so one person sharpens another.
PROVERBS 27:17

The lone wolf is our culture's most enduring stereotype of manhood, and with good reason. Some men do prefer to live in relative isolation. Relationships are risky, so we keep them to a precious few. Developing relational intimacy is nerve wracking, so we keep conversations light. As we move through the stages of life—from living with parents to living alone, school to workforce, neighborhood to neighborhood—the number of associates who are both relationally and geographically close may dwindle to just a few. Or none. When asked to name their friends, it's not surprising to hear a man offer just one or two names, often of guys who live a thousand miles away. Some will respond with, "Um . . ."

Most men don't see this relational deficit as a problem. After all, we're supposed to be able to "deal with it," whatever it is. Another enduring stereotype of manhood is that we don't ask for directions, and that applies to more than navigation. We don't read the instructions that come with a new appliance. We don't go to the doctor unless we can't stand up straight. Talk to a counselor? You must be joking.

Self-reliance is a useful trait in many situations. As the ads for Viagra so charmingly illustrate, it's great to be able to fix your own radiator or start a fire with a flint and a knife. Yet there are times when going it alone makes you weaker, not stronger. Trusted friends are vital for spiritual health.

Few men would score higher on the machismo scale than David, the legendary king of ancient Israel. Warrior, poet, lover, leader—this was a man's man for sure. Fearless in battle, successful in everything he tried, David literally killed a giant. Women actually followed him in the streets singing his praises. Yet David was no lone wolf. He understood the importance of having a close friend and confidant. Jonathan, the son of King Saul, became David's best friend and ally. The two were inseparable companions and trusted one another with their lives. When circumstances forced them apart for what would be the last time, they parted with these words: "Go in peace, for we have sworn friendship with each other in the name of the LORD" (1 Samuel 20:42). The two men embraced and wept and David wept the most (verse 41).

Friendships strengthen us. The men who know us best are able to encourage us most. They hold us accountable, defend us, and offer wisdom. Those who have been part of a sports team, a military unit, or a business startup understand the depth of camaraderie that can develop among close companions, and the value of those relationships. If you have worn the title Lone Wolf as a badge of honor, it may be time to rethink your strategy. As the writer of Ecclesiastes put it, "Though one may be overpowered, two can defend themselves. A cord of three strands is not quickly broken" (4:12). Having a few close friends makes you richer, stronger, and more confident than being on your own.

"Who's your best friend?" I asked my daughter when she was in her teens. She answered without hesitation. "Katie, Emily, Grace, Colleen, Hannah, Sierra, Lindsay, Kelsey, Kaylie, and Liz." She wasn't kidding. When asked the same question, you may not be able to spit out ten names, but it would be great to say something other than "Um."

A TIMELY TIP

Walking with a friend in the dark
is better than walking alone in the light.
HELEN KELLER

TRY IT

Choose an activity you'd like to try
this week, and one friend to share it with.

A PRAYER

Lord, relationships scare me.
I can handle just about anything, but I'm afraid
to get too close to people. Help me to relax.
Give me the courage to open myself to others
so that I can have a true friend—and be one.
Amen.

DAY 21

BELIEVE GOD

THE PROMISE

You are worth more
than what you do.

So God created mankind in his own image,
in the image of God he created them;
male and female he created them.

GENESIS 1:27

"W ell, I guess it's finally over." I heard the words from
an older man who had enjoyed keeping active in
retirement. Occasional calls from former clients had kept him
employed part-time, contributing to his household income
and, more important, to his self-esteem. But the calls had
trickled to a stop. "I guess nobody wants me," he concluded.

That same week I spoke with a young man, dissatisfied with a job that paid poorly and offered little advance-
ment, and frustrated at the lack of opportunity elsewhere.
"I'm going to have to move," he said glumly. "There's just
no work around here." Despite four years of military experience and two combat tours, few employers were interested in
making use of his skills, and fewer would pay a living wage
with benefits.

Robots have taken over much of our work that once
defined our lives, and a good deal of the rest has been shipped
overseas. Many young men emerge into adulthood only to

discover that the world has little use for their labor; it can be bought cheaper elsewhere. Older men are finding that their expertise and experience have been devalued; computers recall information faster and cheaper, and they never make mistakes. The value of a man's contribution in the workplace has declined. Many have been forced from once lucrative careers into lesser valued, lower paid jobs. Many are unemployed, underemployed, or dissatisfied with the work available to them. In a world where we are defined by what we do, what is the value of an unemployed man?

Many men are asking that question right now, and the answer some are hearing is, "Not much." Some hear it from employers who are convinced that human beings are simply a cost to be managed. Others receive that message through subtle signals from a spouse who valued them primarily as a wage earner. Other men communicate that message to themselves because they have made the mistake of tying their value as persons to the value of their labor. That works well when times are good, not so well during a recession.

Here's the good news. God values you for who you are. He has endowed you with eternal worth by creating you in His image. If you were never to earn another dime in your entire life, God would love you, honor you, and value you just the same. You are worth far more than what you do. It's true that God gave Adam and Eve work to do—He set them to tending the Garden of Eden (Genesis 1:15), but that was not to earn their keep or demonstrate their value. God values every human soul just because. And that includes you, regardless of what you earn, even if it's nothing at all. Never surrender your sense of worth to an employer—past, present, or prospective. Refuse to allow others to set the value on your life. The value of your labor may fluctuate with the demands of a global market, but the value of your soul is inestimable. God has created you, and He values you. Nothing can change that.

I chatted with a friend who was forced to retire due to a disability. Often confined to home, he's discovered a new "career" in blogging. His entries are interesting and amusing, and though not a paying job, his work adds value to many lives. "How's it going?" I asked him.

"Well, the pain is pretty bad this week," he said. "But I'm managing. And my daughter is moving back to town next month, so that's exciting. All in all, life is good."

Trust God's opinion of you, but never that of the marketplace. You are always worth more than your paycheck, never less.

A TIMELY TIP

One's dignity may be assaulted, vandalized,
and cruelly mocked, but it can never
be taken away unless it is surrendered.
MICHAEL J. FOX

TRY IT

Today, thank God for whatever
your primary activity may be,
whether it seems monumental or mundane.

A PRAYER

Lord, I want meaningful work to do.
You know that, and I trust You to provide it.
In the meantime, I thank You for the dignity
of my life, the strength of my body,
the clarity of my mind, and the passion in my heart.
I know that You value me far more
than others will, and I thank You.
Amen.

DAY 22
- - -

TRUST GOD

It'll all work out.

Do not be anxious about anything.

PHILIPPIANS 4:6

Twenty years ago, when cellular technology was in its infancy, the smart phone barely on the drawing board, and social media not even a gleam in Mark Zuckerberg's eye, the primary electronic distraction we faced was e-mail. Within a year or two, e-mail went from a novelty to a workplace staple. Some of the guys I knew were getting slammed with forty or fifty messages a day. One, an executive with a major company, said that he never traveled without his laptop, even on vacation. "I have to be wired," he told me. "Too much business takes place on weekends. I can't be out of touch." Another fellow I knew worked for a manufacturing company that did business in Asia. "Sometimes I'll send an e-mail to Hong Kong just before leaving the office, like four-thirty," he said, "and I'll get a response in five minutes. Those guys are working at 4:30 a.m."

Teenagers call it FOMO, fear of missing out, when applied to social media. They don't want to miss out on what their friends are doing or the latest celebrity tweets, so they check their phones obsessively. Men often experience FOMO in regard to work. Decisions are made even on weekends, so they check e-mail on Saturday night just to stay in the loop. Coworkers send e-mail and text messages at all hours, so they get pinged at eleven o'clock at night. It's tough to release *all* control of an important project, so it's tempting to check every inbox once a day while on vacation. Sometimes twice or three times. And men use social media too, and news feeds, and live video, stock prices, and all sorts of things that we simply must stay on top of. FOMO is a ravenous beast. It will consume every moment of the day, every second of attention, every ounce of energy.

This special brand of fear is a type of anxiety, a hybrid of worry about the future and a desire for control. It rises from the expectation we put on ourselves, or allow others to place on us, that we must be always competent, always diligent, always on top of the situation. When we realize the futility of this effort, we try even harder. We work longer hours, send more messages, respond more quickly, empty more inboxes, take more calls, send more texts. It doesn't help. Spending more time on electronic communication in order to be more in control of life is like scratching poison ivy in order to cure it.

The answer? Admit your limitations, get away from the screen, and trust God. Sure, you have to do your job. People do need you. But not every minute of every day. Do what you can, and let God get the rest.

By way of contrast to the two executives I mentioned earlier, I had an e-mail exchange with a young leader a while ago. His career was growing rapidly, as was his family, and I knew that must be placing a tremendous strain on his time. I was surprised when he replied to my e-mail within a few minutes, but I quickly realized it was an auto-response. It read, "Thanks for your message. I check e-mail at 10:00 a.m., 2:00 p.m., and 4:00 p.m., and usually respond within two days. If your message is truly urgent, feel free to give me a call." It wasn't, and I didn't, and I think we both slept better than night.

A TIMELY TIP

The more you pray, the less you'll panic.
The more you worship, the less you worry.
RICK WARREN

TRY IT

Take an electronic Sabbath this week,
twenty-four hours when you
will not go online.

A PRAYER

Lord, there's always one more thing I need to do,
one more message I need to send,
one more crisis I have to manage.
Help! Give me the freedom to relax.
Help me to trust You
for all the details of my busy life.
Amen.

DAY 23

FOSTER KINDNESS

THE PROMISE

Nice guys do finish first.

Blessed are the meek, for they will inherit the earth.

MATTHEW 5:5

I supported myself through graduate school by working in one of the high-tech plants along Massachusetts Route 128, Boston's famed Technology Corridor. Lest you get the wrong idea, let me add that I was studying for ministry at a nearby seminary, and the "high-tech" facility was a manufacturing plant that produced microwave instruments. A factory is a factory, no matter what it produces, and I was a security guard. My job was to walk around once an hour and call the fire department if the place happened to be burning to the ground. Ralph had a different job. I have no idea what his title was. All I know is what he did all day, which was stand in the main corridor next to the cafeteria and make insulting remarks to everyone who walked past. No kidding. "Here comes a real moron," he might say as someone stopped at the vending machine. Or, "Hey doofus, who let you out of the nuthouse? What's up, ——? Yo, —— face!"

I'd love to tell you that I had the temerity to confront Ralph for this behavior, to tell him that people don't deserve to be insulted just for showing up to work, and that "vulgarity is the effort of a weak mind to forcibly express itself," to quote Spencer W. Kimball. But Ralph, in addition to being pretty handy with an insult, was about six-foot-six and weighed maybe three hundred pounds. So rather than confront his boorishness, I tried to stay on his good side, smiled a lot, and avoided him whenever possible. I worked at that plant for two years and felt like a coward every time I walked in the door.

Nearly everyone has a Ralph somewhere in their life, an ill-mannered, aggressive, manipulative jerk whom no one has the guts to confront. Lest you judge those who keep silent too harshly, consider the state of discourse in our society, particularly on social media. It seems that Ralph has taken control of cyberspace and is once again hurling insults at all passersby. Those who speak up against such treatment become its objects. No longer a solo act, Ralph is now abetted by an army of trolls, bringing the power of the herd to bear on any who object to rudeness or insult, or simply ask that others be treated with civility.

Is this simply the way life is? Have the trolls finally won? Are good men forced to either endure insults or join in hurling them? In a word, no. Jesus taught us a different way of being human, and He modeled it. "When they hurled their insults at him, he did not retaliate; when he suffered, he made no threats. Instead, he entrusted himself to him who judges justly" (1 Peter 2:23). Blessed are the meek, Jesus taught, because they win in the end.

When I think about those days at the microwave plant, I do wish I'd found the courage to ask Ralph to tone down the rhetoric. He meant most of it in jest, I'm sure, and may not have known how it was perceived by others. And who knows what inner pain may have driven the poor man to be so caustic. I wish I'd done something to intervene, for his sake and for others'.

Now I guard my own speech much more zealously than I once did. I have been Ralph a time or two in my life, using sarcasm to do what should have been accomplished through gentle conversation. It is perilously easy to be swept along with the drift toward rudeness. I think of that whenever I move the cursor to the SEND button. Ralph won every argument on the shop floor through bombast and bullying. But when all was said and done, he lost the respect of others and perhaps himself.

Nice guys really do win in the end.

A TIMELY TIP

I think it is important that we rebuild
an atmosphere of forgiveness and civility
in every aspect of our lives.

T. D. JAKES

TRY IT

Wear a rubber band around your wrist
for a week and snap it every time
you say something unkind.

A PREAYER

Lord, help me think before I speak.
Sometimes I get so frustrated that I just want
to scream. I'm tempted to trade jab for jab
and insult for insult. I want to do better.
Help me say only things that will make
a positive difference in the world.
Amen.

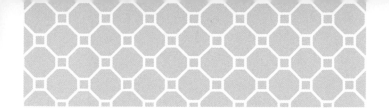

DAY 24

— — —

DON'T QUIT

THE PROMISE

You can handle it.

What, then, shall we say in response to these things?
If God is for us, who can be against us?

ROMANS 8:31

Whend I was a young pastor, a colleague reported a
conversation he'd had with a man in his church. It
seems this fellow had gone to the pastor for guidance. The
problem? The fellow wasn't sure. "Can you tell me why you're
here?" my friend asked.

"I don't really know."

My friend pressed further. Was the man ill? Having
marital problems? Was he mired in debt? An alcoholic? The
answer was no in each case.

"So, what is it you want?" my friend asked, a bit
puzzled, and I've never forgotten the answer. The man said,
"Sometimes I just want to go off in the woods and stay there."

"Are you saying that you want to take your own life?"

"No, not that. I just want to disappear."

My friend and I were both at a loss on how to counsel
the guy. As young preachers, we had lots of book learning
but little life experience. It would be years before I discovered just how common this phenomenon is. Though perhaps

expressed in different terms, the underlying urge is anything but rare. Grown men, once filled with energy and passion, can feel paralyzed by the mountain of responsibilities they face. The result is a low-grade hopelessness that manifests itself in an overwhelming desire to do—nothing.

Life challenges pile up so slowly that you may barely notice them. Then, seemingly all at once, they loom so large as to be debilitating. Debt can be like that. A small balance on the credit card can grow a little, then a little more, until one, two, or even three cards are at their limit. No one student loan seems like a bad decision, but an aggregate sixty-thousand-dollar debt is a lot to pay off, even for a college grad. What can you do? It's tempting to do nothing.

The nagging back is aggravated by a few extra pounds, which in turn inhibits exercise. In a quick minute, you're looking at scales that read a hundred pounds over ideal weight. Giving up one bag of chips won't fix that. What do you do? Maybe nothing.

Relationship problems don't spring up overnight. Like weeds, they grow for a long time beneath the surface, then shoot up an ugly stem. You break it off, and it sprouts again. And again. And again. Before long, weeds are everywhere. What will you do? Probably nothing.

I've always read Romans 8:31 as an anthem against the great evils of the world—persecution, racism, systemic injustice of all kinds. Will the great villains of history wipe out God's people? Paul asks, then shouts a rousing answer to his own question: no way! And that's accurate.

Yet I see here another reading of this iconic verse, one that's more mundane and more personal. What can destroy my psyche, or sap my spiritual energy, or render my life useless and meaningless? Can credit card debt do that? Can a bad marriage? Can a dead-end job and broken-down lawnmower and a mountain of bills and a bum knee keep me from living the vibrant, full life God intends for me? No way!

The challenges before you may indeed be ponderous, but they are not insurmountable. God plus one is a majority in any situation. The mountain you face has been accumulating for months, perhaps years or even decades. But even mountains can be moved. Never lose heart! Never give in! Never give up hope! Your life is a miracle in the making.

A TIMELY TIP

Obstacles don't have to stop you.
If you run into a wall, don't turn around
and give up. Figure out how to climb it,
go through it, or work around it.

MICHAEL JORDAN

TRY IT

Before you end your day today,
and each day, list three things
for which you are grateful.

A PRAYER

Lord, there are days I don't see much hope
for the future. I long to feel energy
and passion again. Help me, Lord,
to see the future as You see it.
Give me faith. Give me hope.
Amen.

DAY 25
- - -
SEEK WISDOM

THE PROMISE

God will help you decide.

If any of you lacks wisdom, you should ask God,
who gives generously to all without finding fault,
and it will be given to you.

JAMES 1:5

Your work schedule is demanding, and your family needs more of your time. Yet you have bills to pay. Having the overtime income makes it easier for everyone. What's the answer?

You believe that sex is reserved for marriage, yet you and your girlfriend are both living on fixed incomes. If you marry, she loses her late husband's pension. Is it wrong to move in together as long as you're truly committed?

You're in the break room at work, and others, including your boss, begin making off-color comments about a female coworker. They ask what you think. What do you say?

A family member's lifestyle is clearly outside the biblical norm, and it's difficult for other family members to accept. They want to break off contact to show the strength of their convictions. What will you do?

You're in frequent contact with a family member who is so plainspoken as to be downright rude. You'd like to give the person a piece of your mind, but others remind you that "love bears all things" (1 Corinthians 13:7 ESV). How should you respond?

Your car broke down, and your credit cards are maxed out. Do you pay for the repair or make the credit payment called for by the contract you signed?

Over the years, I've seen (or faced) each of the situations mentioned earlier. At one time, I had black-and-white answers to each one. "Yes!" "No!" "Of course not!" "You certainly better!" Looking back, I can see the genuine conflict of conscience each person faced. Life is filled with difficult choices, and there aren't always clear-cut answers. There may be competing goods to be gained, and competing evils to be avoided. Even when biblical principles are clear, applying them in the layered, complex situations we encounter in daily life can be challenging. Sometimes there's a gap between knowing what the Bible says and knowing what to do in a given situation. That gap is the need for wisdom.

One of the clearest promises in Scripture is the promise that God will guide our decision making if we seek Him. Thorny problems do have solutions.

Wisdom is an aid to decision making, not an answer in a box. We long for God to make our decisions for us by providing a single, clear-cut option. We crave the "open door" that we must walk through or the "closed door" that signals a clear no. But wisdom is not an answer to a question; it is the ability to discern the answer. God promises to provide that ability. And we are responsible to pray, consult Scripture, take counsel, exercise sound reason, and, finally, make a choice.

And we must be single-minded in our pursuit of wisdom. The dilemmas we face quickly reveal the mixture of motives that nearly always drives our actions. We work hard because we've agreed to earn our pay, but we also like getting credit for a job well done. We donate to charity because it's the right thing to do, but knocking a few bucks off the tax bill doesn't hurt either. Seeking wisdom requires self-examination. To find God's wisdom in any situation, we must inventory and examine impulses, both godly and selfish, that drive us. When our hearts are clear and our minds renewed will we "be able to test and approve what God's will is—his good, pleasing and perfect will" (Romans 12:2).

Your friend is out of work, again, and asks you with boozy breath if it's okay to crash on your couch for a few nights. Do you say yes and risk enabling his behavior, or do you refuse and let him live on the street? I don't know, but I know that God will grant you the wisdom to make this and many other tough choices that will come your way.

A TIMELY TIP

Never make your most important decisions
when you are in your worst moods.
Wait. Be patient. The storm will pass.
The spring will come.
ROBERT H. SCHULLER

TRY IT

Before making a major decision, ask,
"How will I feel about this choice
five years from now?"

A PRAYER

Lord, I don't know what to do.
There are moments when every option seems right,
and others where each one seems wrong.
Yet You know the way. Guide me toward
a sound decision. Help me see myself
and others clearly. Give me wisdom, I pray.
Amen.

DAY 26

— — —

SURRENDER DEEP

THE PROMISE

When your heart changes,
your behavior will too.

*A good man brings good things out of the good stored up
in his heart, and an evil man brings evil things
out of the evil stored up in his heart.
For the mouth speaks what the heart is full of.*

LUKE 6:45

A botanist would call it *silphium laciniatum*, which most people can't pronounce. The common name is compass plant, which most people don't know. It's a weed, common in the midwestern United States and Canada. Compass plants produce a tallish, wiry stem that sprouts little yellow flowers. If you were to see it growing in the ditch or alongside a field, you might mistake it for a black-eyed Susan or yellow daisy. But the flowers are too small, and the sinewy vine looks more like knotted twine than a flower stem. If you found this weed growing on your property, you would certainly mow it or pull it. And in a week or so it would sprout up again. And you would mow it again, or maybe dig down a few inches to get the root. And in a few days, it would be right back. Again and again and again, no matter how often you mowed or how deep you dug, the ugly, ropey vine would come back every time. That's because there are two parts to this hardy little plant. There is the vine, with its flowers, that grows three feet or so above ground. That's the part that makes a mess of your lawn. And there is the root, which grows beneath the surface—to a depth of up to *fifteen feet*. So there's no sense pulling this weed. Without a backhoe, you'll never get to the root. It'll pop back every time.

Human nature is a bit like the compass plant, as most men have already discerned. There is behavior, which is what we say and do, what's visible. And there is the heart, our inner motivations, the roots of our behavior. If our lives were a fresh green lawn, the "weeds" would be behaviors like anger, selfishness, sexual temptation, impulse spending. These are the behaviors we work so hard to eradicate. Like zealous homeowners, we have developed elaborate systems for dealing with the weeds in our lives: counseling, prayer partners, accountability software, behavior modification techniques. And they all help to some degree. It's vital that we place some check on bad behavior.

But like real weeds, these behaviors have deep roots beneath the surface our lives. Their tentacles run to the heart. That's what Jesus meant when He said, "Out of the heart the mouth speaks." Your behavior is simply a reflection of what's inside you. That's why you can control it for a while by sheer willpower, but only for a while. It's like pulling a weed. It's gone for now, but it'll pop back up in a few days. Selfdiscipline alone cannot remove the roots of your behavior. That's something only God can do.

Here's another agricultural term: *glyphosate*. That's the active ingredient in a product called Roundup. Spray a bit of Roundup on vegetation, like compass plant for example, and the plant will absorb it through its leaves. In a chemical action that takes an engineer to fully explain, the chemical is transported to the roots where it prevents the plant from taking in nutrients. So the plant starves to death. Roundup kills it all the way down to the roots.

If you are working hard to avoid lust, control your temper, discipline your spending, or any number of other weeds in your life, bravo for you. But go deeper. Open your heart to the Spirit. Let Him search your motives, confront your hidden selfishness or hurt, and purify you from all unrighteousness. Then you can begin to starve the inner desires that fuel your behavior, not simply regulate the things you say and do. That transformation begins by admitting the truth about yourself to God—and to you. Confession is the road to freedom. Let God change your heart, and your hands will follow. A little Roundup is good for the soul.

A TIMELY TIP

The confession of evil works
is the first beginning of good works.

St. Augustine

TRY IT

The next time you face your most pressing
temptation, pray for deliverance,
then ask, "Lord, help me understand
why my heart longs for this."

A PRAYER

Lord, I don't have enough willpower
or self-discipline or determination to change
what I do, let alone who I am. I give up.
Here's me, all there is to me.
Fix me on the inside. I'm ready.
Amen.

DAY 27

— — —

DO YOUR BEST

THE PROMISE

Doing good work
is its own reward.

Whatever you do, work at it with all your heart,
as working for the Lord, not for human masters,
since you know that you will receive
an inheritance from the Lord as a reward.

COLOSSIANS 3:23–24

I worked at a shoe store while in college. In those days, employees did a bit more than stack boxes and tend the register. We were expected to be salesmen for the product. That meant measuring every customer's feet, recommending certain styles based on customer interest, fetching shoes from the back room, and, get this, putting them on the customer's feet and tying the laces!

That wasn't all. The manager evaluated us on how many accessory items we sold, things like polish, waterproofing, shoe trees, and handbags. Plus, we had to vacuum the floor at closing time, arrange the window displays, and, you won't believe this, clean the restroom. I loved the job because it meant hanging out at the mall all evening. But the work part? Not so much.

One day the manager called me into the stock room where he had a makeshift office amid shelves. We got along well, and I was expecting a debrief on the previous week's NFL games. "You having any problems at school?" he asked.

"Nope," I said cheerfully. "But thanks for asking."

"Anything going on in your family?" he asked. "Are you sick or something?"

"Um . . . no."

"Then why are you acting like such an idiot at work?"

Wow, I hadn't seen that coming. It seems the assistant manager had told the boss I'd been blowing off extra duties and being insubordinate during his absence. I had become bored with the job, which I thought was a bit beneath me. As a result, I felt entitled to a paycheck just for showing up. I was putting in minimal effort, shirking all extra responsibilities, and being downright rude to my supervisor. The boss was not amused.

My face reddened in embarrassment because I knew the report was accurate. I'd let my employer down, a man I genuinely respected. Worse, I'd let the Lord down by not honoring the commitment I'd made when I took the job.

Over the years, I've had the opportunity to do a good bit of challenging, soul-satisfying work. I've been able to preach the gospel, write for publication, participate in disaster relief efforts, counsel people in their grief, and celebrate with them at their marriage. There have been days I was so eager to get to work that I could not sleep the night before. On such occasions, I never wondered, *Why am I doing this?*

Honestly, there have been other times when my professional life seemed a bit like the shoe store, a collection of mundane tasks that seemed a waste of time. "What's the point?" I've asked myself. But then I recall that Saturday in the stock room when I realized that the quality of my work is not a reflection of my circumstances but of my character.

Your work matters to God. That's true whether you're paid too much, too little, or not at all. It's true whether your efforts are applauded or ignored. Your work matters because you matter. You are created in the image of God, endowed with the ability to think, to choose, and to act. The value of what you do is not set by your peers or your employer but by your Creator.

"I like you, Larry," my boss said. "And I want you to enjoy being here. Just put in a good day's work, and we'll get along just fine." That's a great rule for life.

A TIMELY TIP

Working hard is very important.
You're not going to get anywhere
without working extremely hard.
GEORGE LUCAS

TRY IT

Look for a way to improve
what you do at work, even though
you'll be the only one to notice it.

A PRAYER

*Lord, everything I do at work feels pointless,
and most days I want to quit.
Give me a sense of dignity and self-respect
that I cannot find at work. Help me to value
my effort the way You do. Give me joy in doing well,
even the things that don't seem to matter.
Amen.*

DAY 28

— — —

BELIEVE IN YOU

THE PROMISE

You're not a failure,
even if you've failed.

But you were washed, you were sanctified,
you were justified in the name of the Lord Jesus Christ
and by the Spirit of our God.

1 CORINTHIANS 6:11

You wouldn't think a planet could get fired, but that happened to the ninth rock from the sun. Pluto was stripped of its designation as a planet by the International Astronomical Union, which instead defined it as a "dwarf planet." Pluto, which was designated as a planet in 1930, was given a pink slip because it does not meet new planetary guidelines, which say a planet must orbit the sun, be large enough to assume a nearly round shape, and able to "clear the neighborhood around its orbit." Pluto got the boot for missing that third requirement. Its orbit is oblong and overlaps Neptune's. If it's not one thing, it's another.

Some responded to the announcement with a bit of nostalgia. "It's disappointing in a way, and confusing," said Patricia Tombaugh, widow of astronomer Clyde Tombaugh, who discovered Pluto all those years ago. "I don't know just how you handle it. It kind of sounds like I just lost my job," she said.

Some men understand the feeling. They've been reclassified. They were employed but are now unemployed. They were let go because they no longer meet somebody's requirement. Their position was declared redundant, or the budget was cut, or the workforce was downsized. Suddenly they're on the outside looking in. That's the feeling you get when you're fired from a job, or kicked off a project, or have your security clearance lifted. One day you're in, part of the team, a respected member of the group. The next day, you're nobody.

Others get reclassified through their own poor judgment or negligence. They may be fired for cause, divorced for infidelity, or arrested for a crime. It feels as if their lives have been reduced to a checkbox. Have you ever been convicted of a crime, yes or no? What is your marital status: single, married, or divorced? Are you currently employed? Do you currently have health insurance? Have you ever been diagnosed with depression? Have you ever been party to a lawsuit? Answer yes or no. One's identity can shift from one column to the other in an instant.

According to the gospel, however, nobody has the power to reclassify us in any meaningful way. Terms like unemployed, divorced, discharged, depressed, idled, or ex-convict do not define our identity and never will. We are not defined by our past nor by the labels others impose on use. The apostle Paul puts it this way: "Neither the sexually immoral nor idolaters nor adulterers nor men who have sex with men nor thieves nor the greedy nor drunkards nor slanderers nor swindlers will inherit the kingdom of God" (1 Corinthians 6:9–10). Those are some of the labels others will apply to us, but not one of them can stick. For Paul continues, "But you were washed, you were sanctified, you were justified in the name of the Lord Jesus Christ and by the Spirit of our God" (verse 11). That means you have been "reclassified" by God as a new creation. Though you may have been "let go" by others, God will never lose His grip on you. You have a new life. You are a new creation. You are what you are because of Christ, not because of your past.

Patricia Tombaugh summed up her experience of reclassification this way: "I understand science is not something that just sits there. It goes on. Clyde finally said [about Pluto] before he died, 'It's there. Whatever it is. It is there.'"[5] Pluto is what it is, regardless of what any astronomer may say about it. And the same is true for you. You are who you are by the grace of Christ. Others may try to reclassify you, but He never will. Your place with Him is secure.

A TIMELY TIP

You can deal with an enormous
amount of success as well as
an enormous amount of failure
without losing your identity,
because your identity
is that you are the beloved.
HENRI NOUWEN

TRY IT

Cut the tag out of your shirt
to remind yourself that no one
but Jesus has the right to label you.

A PRAYER

*Lord, it feels like I'm in limbo.
My career hasn't gone the way I'd like it to,
and other people don't seem to think
I'm worth much. Help me see beyond
their opinion to read Your approval.
Thank You for giving me
a place in Your kingdom.
Amen.*

DAY 29

SLOW DOWN

You don't have to do it all.

Take my yoke upon you and learn from me,
for I am gentle and humble in heart,
and you will find rest for your souls.
MATTHEW 11:29

If the following excerpt sounds familiar, know that you're not alone. It's a description of the Achiever theme from the Clifton StrengthsFinder profile. Thousands of people share this trait, and it does bring some benefits.

> You feel as if every day starts at zero. By the end of the day you must achieve something tangible in order to feel good about yourself. And by "every day" you mean every single day—workdays, weekends, vacations. No matter how much you may feel you deserve a day of rest, if the day passes without some form of achievement, no matter how small, you will feel dissatisfied. You have an internal fire burning inside you. It pushes you to do more, to achieve more. After each accomplishment is reached, the fire dwindles for a moment, but very soon it rekindles itself, forcing you toward the next

accomplishment. Your relentless need for achievement might not be logical. It might not even be focused. But it will always be with you.[6]

If you're an Achiever, you're likely successful. You may be a leader in your workplace or community. People see you as the guy who can get things done, someone to depend on. And that feels good.

The downside is that you may work a lot. Maybe too much. You feel lazy when you go home at quitting time. You answer e-mail till bedtime. When you're not working on the computer, you're in the garage or the yard tinkering on a project. Your family has given up on asking for your attention; you're always too busy checking that last item off your list.

I know this because it perfectly describes me. Or it did until my son, then about nine years old, asked me to go outside and throw a ball around. "Later," I said, without looking up from the project in front of me.

"Da-ad," he said plaintively. "You always say 'later,' but you really mean 'never.'"

Ouch.

I knew he was right. I had tracked my hours worked not long before and was averaging about sixty per week. As a husband and the father of two small children, that was insane for both my health and my family's well-being. Why was I doing that to myself? Somehow I had become convinced that achieving more would make me worth more to my family, which is odd because they were possibly the only people who loved me regardless of what I did.

The drive within us to achieve, though a good thing, can easily be co-opted by the enemy of our souls. We become convinced that we must do more, contribute more, achieve more in order to be loved by others, even by God. The result is drivenness that goes beyond a healthy desire to provide for our families or to achieve success. It becomes a consuming demand that we prove our worth by doing just one more thing. Jesus puts an end to all that. He calls us to a life of inner peace that comes from knowing that we are unconditionally loved, accepted by God regardless of what we do.

My son's words pierced the bubble of hyper-focus and spoke truth to my soul. I got up from the desk and went into the yard. Starting the next day, I cut more than a dozen hours from my weekly schedule. Though I was still working plenty, it seemed like a walk in the park compared to my previous routine. Nobody noticed except for my wife and kids, who welcomed the change. And I felt relieved and energized.

God loves your zeal. He applauds your ambition. But there is one thing He loves even more: *you*. So relax. You truly have nothing left to prove.

A TIMELY TIP

Most of the things we need to be most
fully alive never come in busyness.
They grow in rest.

MARK BUCHANAN

TRY IT

Schedule an extra day off this month
to do something with the people you love.

A PREYER

A PRAYER

Lord, I just can't seem to stop this drive within me.
I know I work too much, but I love it.
I thrive on it, even though I know it's harming
my health and the people I love.
Give me perspective.
Help me to value the right things.
Amen.

DAY 30
— — —

REFUSE
COMPARISON

THE PROMISE

You don't have to be
like everybody else.

By the grace of God I am what I am.
1 CORINTHIANS 15:10

When I was in the fifth grade, I witnessed a fight on the school playground. It was between Brian Avery, the tallest kid in the class, and Fred Havner, probably the shortest. The fight was brief, probably less than two minutes. And contrary to everyone's expectation, Freddie beat the snot out of Brian. The smaller boy was quick and strong and fearless. He attacked without mercy and didn't let up until several moments after Brian cried uncle. And from that day on, Fred set the standard for maleness for every kid in the class.

All of us seem to have that standard somewhere in the back of our minds. This profile of the ideal man was birthed somewhere in dim antiquity of the human race and has been handed down to every generation since. This archetypal male is virile, violent, plainspoken, muscular, and exists on a diet of rare steak and hard liquor. He works hard, plays harder, and lives by his own moral code, which may be summarized with these words: a man's gotta do what a man's gotta do. This stereotype has been reinforced by countless legends, war stories, and B movies for generations. The only problem with this superlative vision of manhood is that it's pure fiction. No such man has ever existed outside the pages of pulp fiction. True, many of us stand in front of the mirror and practice lines like "Go ahead, make my day" and "I'll be back," but no one other than Clint Eastwood and Arnold Schwarzenegger has ever delivered them convincingly, and who knows how many takes that required?

Like many stereotypes, the masculine myth contains a grain of truth. Some men do have macho swagger and love the smell of napalm in the morning. But that doesn't describe most men. Think for a moment about the men you know. Some of them love golf, some hate it, and a few have never heard of it. Some guys have more hair on their back than most do on their head, and others shave their scalp. Some wear nothing but denim; others prefer pressed suits and wouldn't be caught dead with their shirt untucked. For every guy who watches nothing but football there is probably another who loves romantic comedies. Some men can't bring themselves to say the words "I love you" even to their wives, and others can't shut up about it. There simply is no one-size-fits-all standard for manhood.

While there may be some general traits that are more characteristic of most men than of most women, that's just what they are: generalities. The likes, dislikes, tastes, and temperaments of men differ widely. God made us all male, but He sure didn't make us the same.

That's important to know because it's easy for men in

any stage of life to make the same mistake I made on the playground, which was to equate violent aggression with true manhood. All people, not just men, can embody the virtues of forthrightness, love of justice, and a passion for defending truth. Fearlessness and self-sacrifice are admirable but genderless traits. And rage, sensuality, and arrogance are no more male than they are godly. The sooner we excise them from our vision of manhood the better.

God created you as a unique expression of the male person, on purpose, to be who you are. So be that. Your family might wish you showed a little more emotion, or a little less. They might wish you loved sports a little less, or a little more. But they love you just as God made you. He does too. You're man enough, just as you are.

A TIMELY TIP

Be yourself.
Everyone else is already taken.
AUTHOR UNKNOWN

TRY IT

Make a list of the ten best things about you,
then read it every day this week.

A PRAYER

Lord, sometimes I don't like who I am.
I hate to complain, but I wish You'd made me
smarter, stronger, taller, and more courageous.
Help me to accept the gifts You have given me
without comparing them to anyone else.
Make me comfortable in my own skin.
Amen.

DAY 31

PRACTICE
GRATITUDE

THE PROMISE

God will provide.

Seek first his kingdom and his righteousness,
and all these things will be given to you as well.
MATTHEW 6:33

Our church offered a financial management workshop, and one assignment was to anonymously report the amount of debt in each household, not including business loans or home mortgages. About thirty families had signed up, so I expected a total of perhaps sixty thousand dollars, maybe two grand per family. When the reports were tallied, our little group admitted to holding over $1.2 million in debt, about forty thousand per household. I was stunned. Then I thought a bit more about the financial obligations we all face. Car loans, student debt, credit cards, medical bills—they add up fast. For many people, debt retirement is the largest expense after housing. Making those payments is a tremendous source of stress on wage earners and tension in families.

Debt comes through a variety of circumstances, such as unforeseen expenses and calculated risks. If we're honest, though, we'll admit that much of it stems from the financial pressure we feel to "have it all." My dad grew up with four siblings in a house that was maybe 750 square feet. The house in which I was raised along with two siblings was 1,700 square feet. The average size of a new home today is nearly 2,400 square feet, and it's inhabited by an average of 2.58 people.[7] The expectation of having a larger, newer home is just one of the financial pressures on families. Interestingly, the many changes and opportunities afforded women in our society have taken little financial pressure away from men. The fact that many wives are in the workforce—and earning better wages than even a decade ago—does not mean less financial stress on families. Additional income often leads us to reach for more, taking on more financial stress in the process.

To minds wracked with anxiety over debt and hearts heavy with the burden of delivering more, more, more, Jesus speaks these words of comfort. Drink them in:

> Therefore I tell you, do not worry about your life, what you will eat or drink; or about your body, what you will wear. Is not life more than food, and the body more than clothes? Look at the birds of the air; they do not sow or reap or store away in barns, and yet your heavenly Father feeds them. Are you not much more valuable than they? (Matthew 6:25–26)

Pay particular attention to that last line: "Are you not much more valuable than they?" If God cares for the smallest and most helpless of creatures, how much more must He care about you, who are part of the crowning achievement of His creation? Relax. Stressing about money is both unnecessary and a waste of time. God has promised to provide for you and your family.

Something about this truth makes it a bit easier to break the stranglehold of materialism on our lives. Materialism is the economic version of the deadly vice of comparison. We want the things we cannot afford mostly because other people have them. Yet when we receive what God has provided with a sense of joy and gratitude, we think less about other people and what they possess. We become more content, more joyful, less stressed.

Our study group was able to grasp that concept as we worked through the financial management course. Twelve weeks later, we again reported our level of debt, and it had been reduced by about $190,000. We essentially paid for a house in three months. How? In part by realizing that God has already provided all we really need.

A TIMELY TIP

Look back and thank God.
Look forward and trust God.

UNKNOWN

TRY IT

Go for a full day (or more) without spending
any money, and experience the sense
of freedom it brings.

A PRAYER

---

*Lord, help me to be content with what
You have given me. I'm grateful for food to eat
and a place to sleep. That's all I truly need.
Thank You for all the extras You have provided.
Amen.*

HONOR YOUR WIFE

THE PROMISE

Honor your wife,
and God will honor you.

Husbands, in the same way be considerate
as you live with your wives, and treat them with respect
as the weaker partner and as heirs with you
of the gracious gift of life, so that nothing
will hinder your prayers.

1 PETER 3:7

The open secret among Christian men is that a good number are unhappily married. Few want to talk about this, especially at church where we often pretend that "Everything's great!" Many married people *are* blissfully united, yet others endure lives of quiet loneliness. For some, the romance went out of their relationship years ago and the companionship not long after. Somewhere amid having kids and making a living and keeping two cars on the road, happiness became a casualty of everyday life. Though married, they are living separate lives.

Some couples cope with the situation by bickering over everything from which movie to watch to who left the cap off the toothpaste. Others take their resentment public, talking to everyone who will listen about their spouse's inadequacy. Some simply withdraw. Their relationship knows neither love nor hate, affection nor resentment. This lifestyle is more common than one might think.

What's a man to do in these circumstances? Many debate with themselves, Hamlet-like, whether 'tis nobler in the mind (or more biblical or righteous) to suffer the slings and arrows of an intractable marriage, or to take arms against a sea of troubles and, by divorcing, end them. Though Jesus Himself conceded that divorce is sometimes inevitable (see Mark 10:1–12 and Matthew 19:3–12), it is not part of God's original plan for human life, and we do best to avoid it. And there is hope for a marriage, or any relationship, that's less than perfect. The commitment that brought a couple joyfully together can bind them to one another with equal joy, provided both partners can take their attention off themselves, their needs and frustrations, and place them on the one God has placed beside them. Honor your partner, Peter advised the men in his churches. Treat them with respect and dignity—even, he might have added, when that's difficult to do. Harboring resentment and treating your wife harshly will only hinder your own relationship with God.

The same can be true in any family relationship or friendship. When we focus on our needs and wants, nursing anger against the person who has "wronged" us by being an imperfect human being or failing to meet our needs, we further damage both the relationship and our own spirit. A better way to be reconciled in marriage, family, or friendship is to focus on our own shortcomings and pray sincerely for the well-being of the other.

Peter was a married man and, presumably, qualified to give advice on relationships. His counsel rings true. Peter also knew the power of being loved. After his shameful denial of Christ, Peter slunk off to Capernaum to reenter the fishing trade. If the relationship had been a marriage, this period would have been called a trial separation. Yet Jesus sought out Peter and asked him to reaffirm his love and loyalty. Peter did so. A happy ending. That's the power of grace, which can be shown only to one who does not deserve it. Jesus's unwavering love for Peter seems to shine through the apostle's advice on relationships. It is a hopeful sign for those who feel unappreciated by those who should value them most. To be considerate, respectful, and gracious is the most powerful remedy of all.

A TIMELY TIP

It takes three to make love, not two:
you, your spouse, and God.
Without God people only succeed
in bringing out the worst in one another.

FULTON J. SHEEN

TRY IT

For the next twenty-four hours,
avoid saying anything negative
or critical to another person.

A PRAYER

Lord, sometimes I struggle in relationships.
When I feel hurt, I can react in ways that hurt others.
Help me to treat the people I love with gentleness
and respect so that nothing will hinder
my relationship with them—or with You.
Amen.

DAY 33

- - -

ENVISION
POSSIBILITIES

May the favor of the Lord our God rest on us;
establish the work of our hands for us—
yes, establish the work of our hands.

PSALM 90:17

Two extreme teachings on wealth and ambition have circulated among Christians, both false. One is the gospel of prosperity, which holds that God wants you to be rich and the reason you're not is that you don't have the gumption to name it and claim it. By this way of thinking, there is no ambition so audacious that God won't honor it. Whether you want a million dollars, a Super Bowl ring, or the largest chain of hamburger restaurants on the planet, all you have to do is announce your plan to God and hold on for the ride.

The idea is patently absurd. While God has indeed blessed many people with success, Scripture contains no universal promise of wealth. The prudential wisdom of the Bible, found especially in the book of Proverbs, shows the connection between discipline, hard work, and success. But that's not a guaranteed result in every case. Hurricanes happen, and one could happen to you even if you're prayed up.

The other false teaching about ambition is that God

despises it. By this thinking, God delights in your suffering and sits up nights thinking of new ways to pull the rug out from under you, just to keep you on your knees. He wants you humble, meaning poor as a church mouse and just as low. This, too, is plainly incorrect. To be humble is to have a modest opinion of yourself, not to be poor. And while God does occasionally use difficulties to teach a spiritual lesson—as He did with the Israelites in the desert—His purpose is to build people up, not tear them down.

Even a casual reading of the Bible reveals that God has no problem with strong-willed, competent, ambitious people, provided they honor Him. From Abraham to Moses, Joseph to Daniel, and Job to Solomon, holy history is replete with examples of highly skilled, prosperous men whom God not merely tolerated but actively favored. Each of them served God's purpose in some way, sometimes in a position of great privilege and wealth (think Moses, Joseph, Daniel, and Job), and sometimes in privation or even prison (think Moses, Joseph, Daniel, and Job). The point is not that it's wrong to have ambition, or that it's right. The question is whether one's ambition honors God.

How can you determine that? Here's a simple test. When you ponder your greatest aspiration, what do you see? Many men look into the future and see only themselves—living in a fine home, commanding great authority, being comfortable, wealthy, and respected. Those things are fine in and of themselves, but they make a poor goal for one's life. When your ambition is self-advancement, you likely will not honor God by fulfilling it. As Jesus put it, "What good is it for someone to gain the whole world, yet forfeit their soul?" (Mark 8:36).

If you look into the future and see other people, you may be on track. If your ambition is to see hungry people fed, sick people made well, weary people unburdened through new inventions or processes, the lives of others improved by efficient goods and services, communities transformed through wise governance, it shows that your ambition is about others and not yourself. That's the kind of work God favors.

Moses, the great leader of God's people, was not afraid to pray for God's blessing on his work. He asked for God's favor so that his work might endure. Do you have a grand ambition? Submit your plans to the Lord, then go for it!

A TIMELY TIP

Everyone should try to realize
their full potential.

BARACK OBAMA

TRY IT

Consider this question and share your answer
with a friend: What would you attempt
if you knew for sure you wouldn't fail?

A PRAYER

Lord, I have big ideas, and they won't leave me alone.
My heart is filled with vision and passion,
and I know You put them there.
Show me if I'm wrong, Lord, and bless me
if I'm right. Let me shine bright for You.
Amen.

DAY 34

HOLD ON

THE PROMISE

You'll never be alone.

My family lived in Michigan when I was a kid, not far from Lake Huron. On many a summer day, my mom, my sister, and I would walk along the road to the town beach, popping tar bubbles along the way, then race across the hot sand to dive into the frigid blue of the world's fourth-largest freshwater lake. The Great Lakes never get all that warm, but under the summer sun, the chill was refreshing. The shimmering water appeared calm and cool beneath the bright sky.

One year, long after the leaves had fallen, beyond trick-or-treating but before Thanksgiving, the Great Lakes State enjoyed a warm spell with temperatures spiking back into the seventies. The sudden change was eerie but not unpleasant, and one night after supper our family took a walk to the town beach. We stood in the darkness, my bare feet wiggling into the cool sand. Moonlight shone on the water's surface, now roiled by the autumn wind. Whitecaps broke onto the shore like ocean waves. I inched closer, both fascinated and intimidated by the big water. "Can I go in?" I asked my mom.

"Just be careful."

I inched into the water. To my surprise, it now seemed warm. A wave gushed around my ankles. I took another step, and water surged about my waist, nearly knocking me off my feet. "Larry!" my mother called, and I took another step forward. A massive breaker crashed over me, pushing my legs out from under me. Water flooded over my head, driving me toward the shoreline. Then it stopped, and in the same instant reversed course. I was under the foam now, caught in the undertow of one trillion gallons of raging current, sweeping me into the deep. In that moment, I knew I was lost.

Then the water was gone. I was lying on the beach, the clothing nearly stripped from my body, my mother's hands grasping my left arm. She dragged me, spitting and coughing, to the high-water line and said, "Well, that was some adventure, wasn't it?"

I'll say. Did she know she had just saved my life? Or was that all in a day's work for a mother? Either way, I knew it was only because of her watchful eye and firm grasp that I was not swept away.

I've not encountered an undertow quite like the one on Lake Huron. But since that night, many dark waters have swirled about my head. Disability. Divorce. The death of a child. Unemployment. All of them threatened to pull me under, but in each case I was held firm by the strong hand of God. That's not to say that I never got wet. Pain. Loss. Rejection. Fear. Failure. There is no biblical promise, stated or implied, that we will not face such trials. The promise is that they will not overcome us because God's watchful eye and firm grip will keep us from being overwhelmed.

Here's a firm hand you can hold onto any dark November night: you will never be left alone. When you pass through the waters, God will be with you; and when the flood rushes over your head, you will not be swept away.

A TIMELY TIP

A God wise enough to create
me and the world I live in
is wise enough to watch out for me.

PHILIP YANCEY

TRY IT

Find a quiet place to be alone,
and sit in silence for fifteen minutes,
listening for God to speak.

A PRAYER

Lord, sometimes it all seems like too much.
The problems I face are not small and manageable.
They're like giant waves or rushing winds.
I feel overwhelmed. Right now, I claim
Your promise of presence and protection.
Hold me tight, and never let me go.
Amen.

DAY 35

LEAVE A LEGACY

THE PROMISE

_____

Your life is a legacy.

And the things you have heard me say in the presence
of many witnesses entrust to reliable people
who will also be qualified to teach others.

2 TIMOTHY 2:2

Why, yes, a bulletproof vest." Those were the last words of Domonic Willard, who was executed by firing squad during the Prohibition era. He had been asked if he had any final requests and had the presence of mind to ask for the one thing that might save his life. The quip also gave new meaning to the term "gallows humor." The last words of some other men have been poignant and moving, like those of inventor Thomas Edison, who said, "It is very beautiful over there," just before passing away. Whether he'd caught a glimpse of heaven or was referring, as some think, to the scene outside his window, he left with a lovely thought in mind.

Others have exited the stage on dramatic, even morose, last lines, like film producer Louis B. Mayer, who said, "Nothing matters. Nothing matters." Winston Churchill said, not surprisingly, "I'm bored with it all." Photographic inventor George Eastman wrote, "My work is done. Why wait?" The words were in his suicide note. Last words are often a testament to the value of life. Some find it humorous, some painful, others delightful. "Tell them I've had a wonderful life," said philosopher Ludwig Wittgenstein, surprising friends who knew that he'd suffered many hardships.

Regardless of their outlook on life, nearly everyone seems bent on leaving something behind, perhaps an invention or an inheritance or an accomplishment. The older we grow the more eager we are to establish a legacy. This quest for meaning can be all consuming. Of the 290 people who have died while climbing Mount Everest, how many were working on their bucket list? Sailing solo around the world, making a million dollars, writing a book, running a marathon—many of the things we do are attempts to write "I was here" on the pages of history.

Yet the true legacy we leave, the only monument that can endure, is a life lived for the gospel of Jesus Christ. Though not his literal last words, the apostle Paul left an inspiring final testament in his writings from prison, close to the end of his life. "I am being poured out like a drink offering on the sacrifice and service coming from your faith," he wrote to the church at Philippi (Philippians 2:17). He viewed his whole life, and especially his last days, as a living sacrifice for the gospel. And he wrote to his young protégé Timothy, "What you heard from me, keep as the pattern of sound teaching, with faith and love in Christ Jesus. Guard the good deposit that was entrusted to you—guard it with the help of the Holy Spirit who lives in us" (2 Timothy 1:13–14). It's in your hands now, he told the young man. Take the legacy of my life and teaching, and pass it on to others, who will pass it on to others, who will pass it on to others. That's how a legacy is made.

This is good news for men who find themselves thinking, "Wait a minute. What happened to the 'big thing' I was supposed to be doing?" Family matters and earning a living take much of the time and energy we thought would be invested in building an empire or scaling Everest or at least paying off a mortgage. What are we left with? We're left with the confidence that a life given for others is a more potent legacy than a million bucks or a list of triumphs. A well-lived life is the most treasured testament of all.

And speaking of last words, my favorites are those of Mother Teresa, who died on September 5, 1997. She said, "Jesus, I love You. Jesus, I love You." Whether I knowingly make a last utterance or not, I hope my life will shout those words long after I'm gone.

A TIMELY TIP

The greatest legacy one can pass on
to one's children and grandchildren is not
money or other material things
accumulated in one's life, but rather
a legacy of character and faith.

BILLY GRAHAM

TRY IT

Write the words you would like
to appear on your tombstone,
then order your life to make them true.

A PRAYER

Lord, I want my life to count for something.
Yet the work I do and the money I make seem
nothing more than sand slipping through my fingers.
Help me to live every day as if it were my last
so that the character of my life will outlast me.
Amen.

DAY 36

LEARN FROM PAIN

Son though he was, he learned obedience from what
he suffered and, once made perfect, he became the source
of eternal salvation for all who obey him.

HEBREWS 5:8–9

I sat near the altar, which was a string of low, wooden benches strung across the front of the tabernacle. I sat because I could not kneel, my leg swollen as it was from an arthritis flare. While at a camp meeting in northern New York, I'd attended my first-ever healing service, at age thirty, to pray for a miracle. I'd known about the problem in my joints for a long time, having been diagnosed with arthritis in my senior year of high school. A dozen years, a couple of surgeries, and a truckload of ibuprofen had done nothing to improve my condition. Flare-ups were common. I walked on crutches often, or used a cane. The only alternative was knee-replacement surgery—or a miracle.

Cynthia knelt a few feet away, a woman of perhaps thirty-five years and the wife of a good friend. She'd recently been diagnosed with multiple sclerosis and also sought God's healing power. We prayed, along with many others, that God would reverse the course of our diseases. He'd done it for the man born blind, the woman with constant bleeding, the lame man by the pool, and so many others. Why not us?

After the service, Cynthia and I compared notes on our experience. "I felt nothing," I said. "Well, except the pain in my knee."

"Same here," she reported.

Though it was our first healing service, it was not the first time we had prayed for a cure. Yet my arthritis continued, as did her disease. We received no miracle.

Chronic illness and pain are a reality for millions of people, including millions of Christians. Though we affirm God's ability to intervene in our lives in miraculous ways— and I have known some who received that grace—many of us are left to cope with discomfort or disability, not to mention the creeping effects of age. Healing is a mercy for those who receive it. Is there mercy for those who don't?

There is, and it comes in an unlikely guise. All disease is evil, and I take great care never to declare something bad to be good. Yet I have found that there is profit to be gained in the struggle against pain. In the struggle, we find that God provides strength in our weakness, making the unbearable, well, bearable. Spiritual progress comes after throwing oneself entirely on the mercy of God. And in suffering, we discover the fellowship of pain: community, support, and love shared among those who suffer. Perhaps most important, the promise of release from suffering is understood to its fullest only in the throes of misfortune. Even Jesus learned from what He suffered, the Scriptures teach us. If He did, so can we.

One day, all of this will be over. Jesus will return to reclaim the world, and us with it. Sorrow, pain, disease, tears, and even death will be washed away. And these bodies of ours, broken by time and hard use, will be transformed. *Transformed!* We will be made like Jesus, in His glory; scarred but not disabled, broken but pieced together brighter, stronger, and more beautiful than before. It will happen, and sooner than we know.

I moved away from New York within a year after that healing service. I had one joint replaced a year after that, and then another and another and another, collecting the entire set. Though never healed, I've been graced with the ability to walk and ride a bike and tend my yard with no more than the usual aches and pains.

And I heard some years ago that Cynthia had lost the long battle against her disease. She's in heaven now, sitting at the feet of Jesus, I presume. Or possibly climbing a mountain, a lifelong ambition that had been thwarted by her illness. She's been transformed, you see. Just as I will be someday. And you too.

A TIMELY TIP

No matter how devastating our struggles,
disappointments, and troubles are,
they are only temporary. No matter
what happens to you . . . the resurrection
promises you a future of immeasurable good.

JOSH McDOWELL

TRY IT

Notice someone who is suffering,
perhaps even more than you are,
and encourage him.

A PRAYER

Lord, I am weary of this body of mine.
I'm tired of being in pain, of being held back
by arms and legs that won't do what they should.
I long for healing. And I long more for Your presence.
Teach me the lessons I can learn only
by standing with You in Your suffering.
Amen.

DAY 37

ACCEPT CHANGE

THE PROMISE

Your story isn't finished yet.

There is a time for everything,
and a season for every activity under the heavens.

ECCLESIASTES 3:1

You don't have to know what a midlife crisis is to have one. Presumably, nobody knew what to call this phenomenon before 1951, when the term was coined by Canadian psychoanalyst Elliott Jaques. The concept refers to the crisis of identity and self-confidence that strikes some people in middle age, meaning between the ages of forty-five and sixty-five. Tortured by the idea that their youth and opportunities have been lost, some go a little crazy. They may buy a sports car, or have an affair, or quit their job to become a yoga instructor. Younger people may experience something similar, called a quarter life crisis, when graduation, student loan payments, and the nine-to-five create the perfect storm of adult life. Psychological terms aside, anyone can face tough personal questions when shifting from one life stage to another.

Sometimes that happens because we compare ourselves to others and recognize that they have progressed further in life than we have. When other people graduate from college, have kids, buy a house, get promoted, or take an Alaskan cruise, the rest of us can feel that we're not keeping up. "Why am I struggling to pay off this Geo," we wonder, "when my classmates are driving Audis?"

Sometimes we put the pressure on ourselves by setting benchmarks too difficult to achieve. "I'm thirty; I should be married by now." "I'm forty; how come I don't own my own home?" "I'm sixty, and I should be financially independent."

Let's not forget lost youth. After the twenty-first birthday, each one is a reminder of the march of time. Hair loss, hernias, expanding waistlines: these not-so-subtle signs remind us that the clock moves only in one direction. We're not getting any younger—or slimmer or stronger or sexier. Men react to this realization in varying ways. Some sigh with resignation. Some act out in rebellion. Others buckle down with determination. All are saying, "Not yet! Not me! I'm not ready for this stage of my life to end!"

But is that accurate? Does a change of seasons signal an end, or a new beginning? Solomon observed that there is a time for everything in life. A time to work and a time to rest, a time to be young and a time to be old, a time to be the new kid on the block and a time to be the gray-haired mentor. There's even a time to die. The secret to contentment is not to hold on to the season that is slipping away but to embrace the new time that is upon you.

There is a gift in every season from childhood to old

age. Energy, health, passion: these are gifts to the young. Knowledge, experience, and skill come in middle age. And wisdom, patience, and prudence are the gifts of old age. Embrace the adventure of your life stage, whatever it may be. Young men risk their bodies, pushing themselves to physical limits. Mature men risk their fortune, staking their careers on entrepreneurial ventures. Older men may risk their reputations, saying and doing the things they believe, regardless of the impact on their future. If you have not achieved what you'd hoped by this age, so what? You have gained valuable experience. If others seem more successful or wealthy, who cares? You are not living their story. You are living the story that God has written for you. As one chapter ends, another begins. Welcome the change. God isn't finished with you yet.

A TIMELY TIP

God always prepare us
for the great mission but we are unaware.
All the stages are connected; we must
graciously be fully present in each stage.
LAILAH GIFTY AKITA

TRY IT

Seek out a man ten or more years older
than you and ask, "What should I know
about the next decade of my life?"

A PRAYER

Lord, I'm not ready for this. Things are moving too fast. I want more time to be young, more time to succeed, more time to make my life count. Give me the knowledge that You are in this, that we're doing it together. Help me to learn the lessons from the stage of life I'm in.

Amen.

DAY 38

HOPE FOR HEAVEN

THE PROMISE

There's more to you
than meets the eye.

For we know that if the earthly tent
we live in is destroyed,
we have a building from God,
an eternal house in heaven,
not built by human hands.

2 CORINTHIANS 5:1

Her name was Mrs. Schneider, and she must have been about ninety years old. Maybe a hundred. She was the oldest person I had ever met, which isn't saying much because I was only seven at the time. Mrs. Schneider was our next-door neighbor, which, in rural Michigan, meant that she lived within sight of our house. On long summer afternoons, I would sometimes visit Mrs. Schneider, and we would drink Kool-Aid and play dominoes. My mother encouraged these visits because she knew the old woman needed companionship and that I needed something to do besides throw water balloons at my sister.

I thought Mrs. Schneider was the coolest. She had the most interesting skin, very thin and crinkly. One day she sported a bandage on her forearm that Mom said covered skin tear. I tried tearing my skin, but it just snapped back in place. And she had a plastic box with twenty-one compartments, three for each day of the week, morning, noon, and night. They held her pills, each one brightly colored, like an Easter egg. I wished I could take pills too.

Every now and then Mrs. Schneider would take a break from dominoes to lie back in her easy chair and drape a damp cloth over her forehead. I tried it myself. What fun!

What I didn't know was that Mrs. Schneider was a frail, ailing woman. She passed away later that summer. "That's odd," I thought. "She seemed perfectly normal to me." Yet her body was giving out, little by little and then all at once. It's happening to all of us, despite our best attempts to keep strong and vital. A torn ligament here, a hernia there. A little high cholesterol or low blood sugar or elevated blood pressure, and before you know it you're taking pills with every meal and reaching for a damp cloth to drape over your forehead.

The more active we are the more frantically we deny the evidence of age. Lots of guys play softball for one season too long, or lift the couch when they know they should use a dolly, or go for the layup with their knees and hips screaming, "Noooo!" At twenty-four, we realize we're not eighteen anymore. And that realization comes back at least once a decade. Sooner or later, the body forsakes us all.

Thank God there is more to life. You are not what you see in the mirror. Well, not just that. There is more to you than meets the eye. That person looking back at you is an eternal soul, not destined to perish with the flesh it inhabits. As your body grows weaker, your spirit can grow stronger. And one day it will enliven a stronger, brighter, more durable frame than the one you now see.

I think of Mrs. Schneider occasionally, and others who have passed away, like my grandparents, my daughter, my friend Dennis, some aunts and uncles. Their bodies let them down, as bodies do. But they now inhabit a dwelling not made with human hands. Though they have died, they are alive and well in a new and glorious home.

A TIMELY TIP

Heaven doesn't make this life *less* important;
it makes it *more* important.

BILLY GRAHAM

TRY IT

Ask yourself how you would behave
if you knew today would be your last.
Now live that way.

A PRAYER

---

*Lord Jesus, I can see that this life isn't going
to last forever. You have promised a life
that will never end, and I want that life.
I trust You. I'm placing my full faith in You.
I want to be born again.
Amen.*

DAY 39

DISCOVER
PURPOSE

For whoever wants to save their life will lose it,
but whoever loses their life for me
and for the gospel will save it.
MARK 8:35

How old were you on 9/11? Where were you when the Space Shuttle *Challenger* broke apart seconds after takeoff? Do you remember when Neil Armstrong planted the first human foot on the moon? What were you doing when John F. Kennedy was assassinated? When Pearl Harbor was attacked? Most of us can recall only one, perhaps two, of those events. Some know them only from history class and perhaps not at all. Yet each was a defining moment for its time. Each occasion, whether grand or tragic, inspired a generation and infused their lives with something more vital than breath: purpose.

As those signal events recede further into memory, many people feel an acute lack of purpose. We live in a time when many, perhaps most, people have a deep, unsatisfied longing for meaning. "What on earth am I here for?" is the defining question of this century. Though we have unprecedented opportunities, we find little value in them. Despite our access to education, travel, and employment, nothing seems urgent or inspiring. That makes it tempting to pour our energy into petty disagreements about sports or politics. When nothing seems worthy of our loftiest ambition, trivial things capture our attention. This lack of meaning produces a soul ache that drains a bit of life from us each day. Even our toys and games seem pointless.

One reason we struggle to find purpose is that we look for it in the wrong places, usually within the narrow confines of our own heart. When we ask, "What's the purpose of my life?" we really want to know something like this: What will make *my* life better? What will make *me* happier? What will hold *my* attention? What would make *me* wealthier or better known or more comfortable?

The common denominator is the self. By asking, "What is the purpose of *my* life?" we fall into the ravine of despair that Jesus warned His disciples about. For by holding tightly to our own dreams, wants, and needs we lose the very life we long to redeem. Purpose will never be found in doing something to make our own lives more exciting or interesting. Satisfaction cannot be found in serving oneself. Those who try find themselves emptier and lonelier than before.

Where, then, is purpose? It is in surrendering our lives to someone or something else. We find meaning by
lives in service to something far greater than our own glory.

The purpose of a pen is to write. It does not exist for its own sake. It serves the will of another. The purpose of a nail is to bind boards together. It is worthless until bashed on the head and driven from sight. The purpose of a life is to serve God by serving others. Your greatest achievement, the thing that will bring you the deepest sense of satisfaction and fulfillment, will never be something so shallow as making more money or having more leisure time. Such things are not wrong, by any means. They simply lack the power to satisfy because they serve only the self. Your true purpose lies outside yourself. You will find it by giving yourself away.

A TIMELY TIP

Learn to light a candle in
the darkest moments of someone's life.
Be the light that helps
others see; it is what gives life
its deepest significance.

ROY T. BENNETT

TRY IT

Make a list of the ten greatest needs
you see around you,
then choose one to help meet.

A PRAYER

Lord, some days I wonder why I'm here.
I find no meaning in my work or my play.
Yet I know You created me for a reason.
Show me the work You have for me to do.
Amen.

DAY 40
— — —

KEEP THE FAITH

THE PROMISE

God is writing a better story
for your life.

*And we know that in all things God works
for the good of those who love him,
who have been called according to his purpose.*

ROMANS 8:28

I wrote a book called *When Life Doesn't Turn Out the Way You Expect*, so you'd think I would find life unsurprising. I thought so too, at that time. My coauthor had survived a brain tumor. I'd had knee replacement at a young age and lost an infant child. We thought we were experts at dealing with loss because we'd done it. But life's capacity to startle is not diminished with age. After writing that book, I was divorced, disappointed by a friend, changed careers, and had three, yes, three more operations. If life was surprising before, it's been a fun house since!

Many people find life surprising. Perhaps most of us thought we'd have stellar careers, perfect health, great marriages, and model children. And some do. But life is not a whip we can crack at will. It's a river that takes its own meandering course, and takes us along for the ride. Thankfully, there are long, lazy stretches of flat water. Yet rapids and waterfalls are there too.

After yet another unexpected turn in my life, an old friend and wise pastor gave me this advice. He said, "Larry, a chapter in your life has come to a close, and there's nothing you can do about that. You're sad now because you don't understand what it means. That's because you don't get to write the chapter titles for your own life story. Only God can do that. For now, step into the next chapter with gratitude and wonder. As you look back, you'll see that God has written a meaning over this stage of your life. Perhaps it will be 'Grace' or 'Growth' or 'Humility.' In time, you'll understand. Till then, accept that God is moving you further along in the story He is writing for your life."

Few people understand the meaning behind the sudden turns life takes when they come. Some claim to see a perfect correlation between every circumstance and a seemingly simple lesson God is teaching them. Perhaps they're right sometimes. But more often it seems that God uses the tensions and troubles, victories and defeats—even the pain—to write a long, long story that cannot be fully understood in Acts I or II. You must read all the way to the end to understand the meaning of this tale that is your life.

Think of the great men of the Bible, and you'll see this played out. Abraham's life was an epic that played out over a century. He began in Ur, migrated to Egypt, and settled in Canaan. He was childless for decades, then blessed with a son, then called upon to sacrifice that same beloved child.

Abraham's life was anything but predictable, yet he became a model for all who believe. His great-grandson Joseph had an eventful life, too, and not according to plan. Born as a favorite child, sold into slavery by his brothers, jailed on a false accusation, elevated to prime minister of a nation, reunited with an aged father—Joseph's life was an odyssey of reversals of fortune. And at the end, he was able to say to the brothers who had betrayed him, "You meant evil against me; but God meant it for good" (Genesis 50:20 ESV). The many changes in your life will serve a purpose, too, if you'll keep reading to the end of the story.

Keep the faith, brother. Keep hoping. Keep trusting. Keep on seeking God and pursuing holiness and following Jesus as best you can. God is writing the story of your life, and you won't believe how it turns out. Spoiler alert: it's a happy ending.

A TIMELY TIP

When you're going through hell,
keep going.
WINSTON CHURCHILL

TRY IT

Draw a horizontal line on a sheet of paper
to represent your life. Next, mark every
point at which God has intervened,
and thank Him for these moments.

A PRAYER

Lord, I've been working hard and doing my best,
but nothing seems to have turned out
the way I planned. I'm disappointed, sometimes
angry. This isn't the life I signed up for.
But I trust You. Help me to keep on trusting
until the day I finally understand.
Amen.

MY PRAYER FOR YOU

Now this is my prayer for you, that you may have unwavering confidence in God and in His love for you; that you may know that your sins are forgiven and that you may be free not only from the guilt of sin but also from the deadly grip of sinful habits; that you may be confident in the man God has created you to be so that you are strong but not arrogant, humble but not fearful, and confident but not unkind; that you may be transformed by the Holy Spirit so that you are truly righteous; that you may be skilled in your work, wise in decision making, generous in giving, and hopeful for the future. Let this be so, in the name of Jesus Christ our Lord.

NOTES

Day 4

1. Charles Dickens, *A Christmas Carol and Other Stories* (New York: The Modern Library, 2001), 22–23.

Day 8

2. "Sorting Through the Numbers on Infidelity," *Weekend Edition Sunday*, National Public Radio website, July 26, 2015, www.npr.org.

Day 10

3. The "Serenity Prayer" by Reinhold Niebuhr (1892–1971).

Day 14

4. Corrie ten Boom, "Guideposts Classics: Corrie Ten Boom on Forgiveness," *Guideposts* website, July 24, 2014, www.guideposts.com.

Day 28

5. William J. Kole, "Dinky Pluto Loses Its Status as Planet," The Associated Press, website of *The Washington Post*, August 24, 2006, www.washingtonpost.com.

Day 29

6. "Clifton StrengthsFinder Themes," Gallup, Inc., 2012, www.gallup.com.

Day 31

7. U.S. Census Bureau, "Median and Average Square Feet of Floor Area in New Single-Family Houses Completed by Location" and "Households and Families: 2010," www.census.gov.

ABOUT THE AUTHOR

LAWRENCE W. WILSON believes in the power of God to transform lives. He's been a pastor, author, editor, ghostwriter, husband, and father. His writing is focused on the intersection of authentic faith and real life. Previous books include

The Long Road Home
Why Me? Straight Talk about Suffering
When Life Doesn't Turn Out the Way You Expect
A Different Kind of Crazy

Visit Lawrence at
WWW.LAWRENCEWILSON.COM

IF YOU ENJOYED THIS BOOK, WILL YOU CONSIDER SHARING THE MESSAGE WITH OTHERS?

Mention the book in a blog post or through Facebook, Twitter, Pinterest, or upload a picture through Instagram.

Recommend this book to those in your small group, book club, workplace, and classes.

Head over to facebook.com/worthypublishing, "LIKE" the page, and post a comment as to what you enjoyed the most.

Tweet "I recommend reading #PromisesAndPrayersForMen by @Lawrence Wilson // @worthypub"

Pick up a copy for someone you know who would be challenged and encouraged by this message.

Write a book review online.

Visit us at worthypublishing.com

twitter.com/worthypub

instagram.com/worthypub

facebook.com/worthypublishing

youtube.com/worthypublishing